The Food Conspiracy Cookbook

How to Start
a Neighborhood Buying Club
and Eat Cheaply

By Lois Wickstrom

Drawings by Sara Raffetto

101 Productions
San Francisco
1974

ERIC!

Dedicated to the farmers and small businessmen
who taught us the real power of the people.

The "how to eat it" sections of this book would not have been possible without the recipes
contributed by: Sharyn, Bo, Sandi, Eric, Grandma Morris, Criss, Lillian, Elizabeth, Cynthia, Selina,
Allene, David, Walt, Lilia, Susan, Jae, Jean, Vijaya, Joyce, Nancy, Joan, Babbie, Louise, Eloise,
RoRo, Auntie Barrett, Reggie, Jeff, Barbara, Annie, Helen, Brenda, David, Peking Man Commune,
Bee, Emily, Florie, Leo, Flieg, David, Erica, Jean, Marcy, Norma, Lester, Mike, Betsy, Mr. Petroff,
Desmid, Ida, Irene, Margaret, Donna and Birgit.

Second Printing, October, 1974

Copyright © 1974 by Lois Wickstrom
Drawings © 1974 by Sara Raffetto

Printed in the United States of America

Published by 101 Productions
834 Mission Street, San Francisco, California 94103
Distributed to the book trade in the United States by
Charles Scribner's Sons, New York, and in Canada
by Van Nostrand Reinhold Ltd., Scarborough, Ontario

Library of Congress Cataloging in Publication Data

Wickstrom, Lois, 1948-
    The food conspiracy cookbook.

    1. Cookery. 2. Cooperative societies—United
States. 3. Marketing (Home economics) I. Title.
TX715.W636   641.3   73-91940
ISBN 0-912238-45-3

Contents

The Berkeley Food Conspiracies 5

How to Start a Conspiracy 10

Produce/How to Do It; How to Eat It 15

Cheese and Milk/How to Do It; How to Eat It 32

Eggs and Chickens/How to Do It; How to Eat It 48

Beef and Lamb/How to Do It; How to Eat It 62

Fish/How to Do It; How to Eat It 72

Grains/How to Do It; How to Eat It 80

Beans/How to Do It; How to Eat It 105

Nuts, Seeds and Dried Fruit/How to Do It; How to Eat It 112

Herbs and Spices/How to Do It; How to Eat It 121

Conspiring to Buy Non-Food Items 127

Licenses/Keeping Records 129

Index of Recipes 138

The Berkeley Food Conspiracies

When a group of people want to buy food cheaply, but don't want to pay rent or salaries or have a store and are all willing to work, they have a food conspiracy. Buying club and co-op are other names for this kind of organization, but they also apply to groups with paid managers, store fronts and profits.

The food conspiracy movement includes people who want an alternative to supermarket shopping and desire direct control of the kind and quality of the food they eat, as well as its price.

The first food conspiracy started in Berkeley, California, two months after the People's Park struggle. It has subsequently spread to many large cities and among people of all economic backgrounds.

In July, 1969, three Berkeley residents—Vivian, Jim and Anita—met in Vivian's backyard simply to figure out how they could buy food cheaply. Jim knew about the farmers' market and had a VW bus. Vivian knew about organic food. Anita knew how to formulate questions and organize. To enlist others to join them, they started writing blurbs in people's papers and putting out pamphlets entitled variously "eat to conspire" and "conspire to eat." A sign was posted near a grocery store in the student neighborhood, notices were placed in People's Park bulletins and in the Tenant's Union Newsletter and soon there was a group of us.

At first all we got was produce. One member who owned a pickup truck drove out to the farmer's market every week and distributed food from a driveway. Within six months there was more food ordered than his truck could handle and there were more members than could comfortably fit into a living room for meetings. So on December 1, the conspiracy split north and south. South got the pickup truck. So, here were North's members, organized, facing their first problem: Who is going to get our food?

The Berkeley Food Conspiracies

The solution was one that we forgot many times and had to relearn the hard way, but is the only one that works: *rotation of jobs*. Everybody works. In retrospect it is amazing that we hit upon this solution as early as we did. We were so used to people doing things for us that it didn't seem wrong to let someone do the same job over and over again, so long as he didn't complain. Even two years later we were still being surprised when a key figure succumbed to the burnout phenomenon —suddenly quitting after doing a job too long. We had yet to learn about breaking jobs down into their smallest possible parts and spreading out the work, in order to minimize the chances of burnout. Towards the end of the second year, many of us went to the opposite extreme and decided that each member should learn all the jobs. This didn't work either. First, not everyone owns or can drive a truck and no one wants to loan his truck to a learner. Second, some people have their own gardens and don't buy conspiracy produce—why should they do the run? Also, many of us had small children and it's not easy to get a sitter at three in the morning in order to do a produce run. Similar arguments apply to all the other jobs. We found the best compromise to be: "Him that works not shall not eat—but some work harder than others."

Shortly after the December split, each conspiracy split twice again and then there were eight, each with total autonomy, but most chose to buy jointly with the other groups. We were also expanding from produce into other food items.

Nancy found a cheese shop willing to sell to us in bulk at a small markup over cost. Savings and quality in over 40 varieties caused the cheese run to grow huge in a short time. The Friday night cheese-cutting session began spilling over into early Saturday morning; there was so much cheese to cut and nibble.

Norm started a dry foods distribution of 15 items (oatmeal, brown rice, etc.). He had assumed that he could just bring the food and some scales down to the People's Office (our informal headquarters for all the conspiracies) at a specified time and that we could all weigh out our food and go home with what we had ordered. There was a 10 percent markup to cover spillage and mistakes. That run lost money. The scales weren't balanced and no one tried to weigh accurately anyway. The orders had been added incorrectly and people who hadn't ordered in advance came to pick up food. After several runs with similar results, Norm was $200 in the hole and most members were having to go to the store to buy the food that they had ordered from the conspiracy, and in some cases were not getting their money back. Dry foods, thereafter, were distributed in backyards, garages and churches, with only those who ordered knowing the location. All food was bagged before the pickup, the markup dropped to five percent and dry foods showed an occasional net gain.

In December we were televised. Until then, we had felt safe in our anonymity from a crackdown by authorities. Our generation's experience with the government did not lend us to expect to get away with so radical a step as bypassing stores. We were surprised and nervous when Connie Martin of the U. S. Food and Nutrition Service saw the broadcast and called John to ask if the conspiracy was, or would like to be, authorized to accept food stamps from members. John brought up the topic at the next meeting where it was voted down as too much hassle. However, two members from the soon-to-be-formed Albany Conspiracy, who thought food stamps were worth the trouble, decided to get an authorization themselves and shortly thereafter other conspiracies had food stamp authorizations.

About the same time we started learning about the need for permits and licenses. We discovered that we couldn't buy sesame seeds, flour or beans from a supplier unless we had a resale permit to collect sales tax, even though in California food isn't taxable. Three conspiracies got resale permits. Then the State Board of Equalization, which gives out the tax numbers, told our respective cities about us and some of the cities asked us to buy business licenses. We bought them, of course. We try to cooperate with the government so that they see fit to leave us alone.

In early 1970 the period of leaders began. Gail started all-conspiracy produce and brought crunchy granola down from Davis. Allene and Tony organized fertile eggs and organic chickens. Late in 1970, Eric and Lois, and later Bob and Debby, organized dry foods on an all-conspiracy basis. Eric, Lois, Tony and David set up all-conspiracy caselot (cases of non-foods of all sorts and canned foods). Beth arranged rotation of milk jobs, now that the orders no longer fit into one station wagon. Lois found a supplier of milk in glass bottles who would sell to us at wholesale prices. Gary, George and Lil started a dairy distributorship to serve the conspiracies and bought a refrigerated truck.

Meanwhile dry foods was becoming very big, over $4000 per run. Since some computer time was available to us, Lenny worked out a highly detailed computer program to add up the order, print bagging lists and tags, tell us how much to pay for food and where to buy it. After the shock of finding computers in a people's organization, each member was taught how to fill out his order on a set of IBM cards; Lenny and the computer did the rest. But then the reading machine broke and we found ourselves with a $9000 order to collate by hand. Lenny was too busy handling all the other details of the run to fix the machine and was too burned out

The Berkeley Food Conspiracies

to ever try it again. Now all the jobs are carefully split up so that no one will ever have to do that ghastly a job again.

Gail, too, was getting burned out running produce all this time. So Darryl, Randy and Tom learned how to do it and taught others. The people running caselot were getting tired of all that work also, so Tony wrote down thorough instructions on how to run it and did one run with Mike who did one run with Ted and the rotation continues. After two and one-half years of steady orders without bouncing any checks, we were allowed store status at the Associated Cooperative warehouse in exchange for $900 in advance capital. (The money was raised by loans from members, paid back with six percent interest out of our markup.) This arrangement meant lower prices and delivery.

There are lots of reasons to join a food conspiracy. There are those who live in communes for whom joining a conspiracy is as natural as making soup in a 10-quart pot. There are those who want organic food and cringe at the prices in the health food stores. There are others who just want cheap food or want out of the packaged way of life. We are all in it together.

It is possible we could disappear tomorrow, but that is one topic that never comes up for debate. Someone can announce that he is quitting his job and know that someone else will make sure that the job gets done.

However, there are perennial disagreements. We constantly analyze our suppliers on the basis of price, organicness and lifestyle, choosing those who best fill our requirements. At one point it was even suggested that we should hire a San Rafael commune to run our dry foods and another time that we should open a store. We stand firm in our commitment to support small farmers and businessmen. One thing we know is that we will continue to exist, improvements and setbacks come as they may. There are very few reasons left why any of us ever need to spend money at a local store. If you can't get it through the conspiracy, you can usually get it used.

Just as we have changed Berkeley with our 2000 members and 60 conspiracies, the conspiracy has changed us. Many of us have sold our cars and now drive vans and trucks. Some of us now use herbal medicine and even deliver our own babies. Some of us have gotten more political, others less. We are all much more conscious of how we spend our money and where we spend it. We had a labor-gift exchange in which all skills were filed so that those who could plumb or do wiring or replace windows could contact those who could sew, cook, garden or help move furniture. Buying food with your neighbors is just a start. Sharing food with your neighbors leads to a community.

How to Start a Conspiracy

You don't need your grocery store. Grocery stores take up at least four hours a week of the average adult eater's time, and in return numb his mind with background music, tempt his pocket with end-aisle displays, lure him with advertisements and make him walk past thousands of items he doesn't want in order to find the few he came to buy.

Grocery stores stock things you know you shouldn't eat, but buy anyway because you saw them advertised and want to try them, your kids nag for them or you have low blood sugar because you forgot to eat before shopping. If you were sending someone to shop for you or even if you were showing a shopping list to a neighbor, you probably wouldn't list these items. But once you are in the store with your mind numbed by background music you buy them.

Grocery stores are sneaky. They lure you in with newspaper and radio ads which offer "loss leaders" (items sold at or below wholesale cost). Their managers know that once you are in the store and have bought your mayonnaise, white sugar, white flour, coffee and canned milk (sale items which provide no profit), you will probably also pick up some frozen foods, cake mixes, snack foods or even nonfoods like film and shaving lotion. It is the profit on these latter items that pays for running the stores, for the ad that got you there and the background music that kept you there long enough to buy that candy bar, women's magazine and soda pop that weren't on your shopping list. The profits on these "impulse buy" items are so great that they make up for the loss on the advertised items.

The average dollar you spend at the grocery store represents 80 cents wholesale cost and 20 cents margin (you would call this 20 cents a 25 percent markup). Of the 20 cents, 13 cents goes for labor, 5 to 6 cents for rent, utilities and trading stamps (1-1/2 cents), leaving 1 to 2 cents actual profit.

A grocery store makes its money through volume. A look at the till won't tell the shopkeeper whether all the money in it came from "loss leaders" or from "high margin" items. He hopes it was a mixture of both. A standard shopkeeper's joke goes: "We've got to stop carrying that item, it's losing us money." "Yes, but look at the volume it's doing." Anyway, if the wholesale cost on an item goes up from 80 cents to $1, the retail price usually goes from $1 to $1.25. You may say "look, the grocery store just ate another nickel." But the manager thinks he must do this to keep his margin the same. He knows that the higher price will decrease sales and he'll need those nickels to make up for the loss of volume. We don't mean to declare a "Feel Sorry for Grocery Store Managers Week," but rather to tell you how you can take advantage of the crazy system. You can buy the "loss leaders" and avoid the temptation of the thousands of other items that provide the store's sustenance. Stores can afford a few customers doing this, but if enough people try it they will have to change their ways. If shopping specials appeals to you, by all means, do it. Nobody in the world can beat the price of a loss leader. If, however, you would like a wide variety of foods, including some that are too expensive for you now like nuts and dried fruits or if you want higher quality, fresher food than can be found in most grocery stores, for less money, and no more time than you now spend in the grocery store, then you should start or join a food conspiracy.

After reading this book you will never have to enter a grocery store again. You may decide to do so during moments of laziness, but you won't be dependent on the store for your daily food. Once your conspiracy is going, months might go by without your noticing that your favorite grocery store has closed.

You see, stores are only middlemen between you, the shopper, and their warehouses. Warehouses, in turn, are middlemen between stores and packagers, who again are only middlemen between warehouses and farms. Farmers are middlemen between seeds and food; the seed growers are middlemen between nature and organized planting. All these middlemen go to make up the wholesale price to which the grocer adds his 20 percent margin. You with your neighbors need only to decide how many middlemen you wish to skip.

Not only will you save money, you will also learn how our structured society works, and you will discover how much power a few people with pooled money and energies can have.

All you really need to start is five families, one large car, truck or van, a money can and an accurate scale. (A used baby scale, which can be picked up at a hospital or junk shop for $5 or less, is good.) A place to post notices is useful, too. You and

How to Start a Conspiracy

your fellow members will need to trust each other to spend money wisely and not to lose it. At first if the group is small, it is not necessary to have a bookkeeper. Just trust that everyone will put the right amount in the money can. There isn't a conspiracy we know of that folded due to mistakes made at the money can. It is also a good idea not to have over 50 families in one conspiracy. If yours gets that big, it is time to split into two or more groups.

Rotation of jobs among members is the key to a conspiracy's success. Everyone signs up for a new job each week so that after a few months everyone can do everyone else's job and any member could start a conspiracy if he moves to a different area. There should be no "general managers," "bosses" or hierarchy of any kind. The most common problem the conspiracies have had is one-person-doing-all-the-work. If that occurs, the conspiracy will fall apart when that key person quits or moves. More important is the obvious fact that it is not fair to take advantage of one person. In our experience, if something needs to be done, someone will come from somewhere to do it.

It is essential to point out here that no member of a food conspiracy should ever receive a salary. It may seem rather harmless at first to pay someone a small salary, but you will soon see that no one feels comfortable working as a volunteer next to someone who is paid. Your conspiracy would rapidly become a buying service and then fold.

The first food most conspiracies get is produce. Produce is bought at a farmers' market or produce terminal or occasionally from private farmers. There are three basic ways to distribute the food. You can take specific orders and buy exactly what is specified. Or you can take a given amount of money and buy only what looks good and cheap and divide it equally into boxes for each family. Or you can display the crates of food in somebody's yard, post prices, and let members take what they want. All three ways work; the latter two save the most money.

Cheese is also easy to buy in bulk. Locate a small dairy or cheese store that will give you a discount on 5- to 10-pound blocks or wheels of cheese. Until your conspiracy is fairly large, however, everyone must want the same few cheeses or large amounts of different ones. If there is more than one conspiracy in your area, you might join together to buy quantities of cheese from wholesalers.

You might also be able to convince a store manager to sell you cases of foods like peanut butter, at slightly above his cost. He may even tell you where his wholesaler is and you could buy directly from there. Or look in the yellow pages under "foods—wholesale."

The variety of things a conspiracy can buy is unlimited. We have gotten film, soap, shampoo, kitchen equipment, pet food, clothing, books, dried fruit, nuts, spices, milk, honey, rice, beans, flour, hardware and car parts. Some of these items require permits and licenses which we will discuss later. The first thing to do is get started and then add permits and licenses as you need them. Some conspiracies have gone on for years without any permits. If your conspiracy isn't the first in your area you may never need any permits at all; if one conspiracy gets licensed to the hilt, it can act as a miniature wholesaler for the others. You will also need a license if you want to accept food stamps from members.

MEETINGS

Most people hate meetings, but they are necessary. The most painless time to hold them is just before the food is distributed. That way everybody is there and meetings are guaranteed to be short. You should discuss problems and projects and sign up for next week's jobs. You can discuss community problems as well as food problems. You'd be surprised what a group of five families can do to keep a freeway from going through their homes.

MARKUPS

Since food is so cheap at the wholesale level, you might consider a temporary markup to raise money towards buying something that all the members want, like a scale or used refrigerator. This will not impair the value of your conspiracy as a source of cheap food. It's also a good idea to build up a kitty of about $20, so your conspiracy can stockpile items like toilet paper and light bulbs when they go on sale. Some conspiracies charge a membership fee of $2 per eating adult so that there is always a kitty. Some conspiracies reimburse members for phone, gasoline and bridge-toll expenses; if yours does this, be sure to put a markup on top of your prices to cover the outlay.

MEETING THE PUBLIC

It's probably best not to call yourself a "food conspiracy" when dealing with the establishment. They may not know what you are talking about and it sounds "dangerous." If anyone in officialdom asks what you do, tell them that you are a "buying club" or "co-op" and that you sell groceries, housewares and sundries. When dealing with businessmen, do not tell them that you are nonprofit; they might not sell to you. Tell them you have a markup. They don't need to know that it may be as low as one cent per person to cover some toll calls and a postage stamp.

REMEMBER

Conspiracies only work if all who benefit take an active part in its working and decisions. Mistakes will be made. Conspirators are not professionals. They are just your neighbors collectively trying to make this alternative work. So, if things are delayed at first, remember that conspiracies work by cooperation and be tolerant of your neighbors. Soon it will be your turn to try each job.

Produce

Organically grown produce doesn't taste different from "regular" produce. However it is usually fresher and thus tastes better. Most organic farmers pick their produce at the proper ripeness and bring it directly to the market, so that nutrients and flavor are not lost during cross-country trucking and while sitting on store shelves. Natural fertilizers are also likely to produce food with a higher nutritional value than plants fertilized by chemicals.

The best place to buy fresh and possibly organic produce is your local farmers' market or produce terminal. To find the one nearest you, look in the yellow pages under "fruit and vegetables wholesale" or ask an employee at a store where you like the produce. You may want to check out several markets in your search for the best food for the least money. The best time to go is on a weekday at five or six in the morning.

To find out what the food should cost write the Consumer and Marketing Service of the U. S. Department of Agriculture, Washington D.C. 20250 (or call your local USDA branch) and ask to be put on the mailing list of the Daily Produce Bulletin for your area. This service is free. Every day, if the U. S. mail does its job, you will be sent a listing of the fruits and vegetables in season and the going price for them. It will also tell how many pounds or items to expect in a case or crate. This information will protect you if sellers try to overcharge you, thinking you won't know the difference. The sellers will be impressed that you do know the correct prices and after a while may offer you special deals. (The listed prices do not necessarily apply to organic produce.)

You may have to try several produce sellers before you find one who wants to deal with you. When you do find one who will give you good prices and in general is nice to your members, give him as much of your business as possible. He in turn will

Produce/How to Do It

cut prices for you when he can. You may also consider helping farmers harvest their crops in exchange for a discount.

ORGANIC PRODUCE

If your conspiracy is interested in buying organic produce, investigate the seller's claims that his produce is organically grown before you buy. You should not be convinced by signs on the growers' booths alone. The points to cover include the following:

• Ask what each "organic" seller puts into his compost pile. If he says "What compost pile?" or "Oh, everything" be suspicious. A compost pile is a pile of all non-diseased stalks, vines and manure accumulated on a farm. Often calcium- or phosphate-bearing rocks are thrown in. The mixture rots and makes good free fertilizer.

• Ask what fertilizers each farmer uses. Compost, manure, lime, ashes, fish emulsion, mulches of rock and/or hay, leaves, sawdust, etc. are all good natural fertilizers. Chemicals only contribute to the deterioration of the soil.

• Ask what each farmer does about pests. There are natural predators available. It is also possible to give plants enough nutrients through mulches and natural fertilizers so that the bugs are no longer interested. There are also certain varieties of plants that simply do not interest bugs.

• Ask the farmer if he takes advantage of companion planting. Some plants help each other grow. Lettuce and radishes will improve each other's health and productivity if planted near each other. Other plants will ward off bugs; garlic and marigolds are particularly good at this.

• If you are feeling ambitious, ask if you may go out to see the farm. While you are there take a sample of the soil for testing for nutrients and DDT and other chemicals. Soil-test kits for nutrients cost about $5, and any chemistry student can perform the DDT test. DDT also stays in the ground for a number of years, so ask how long the land has been free of DDT and similar chemical abuse. In Berkeley we even went so far as to investigate buying a gas chromatograph for DDT testing, but this plan fell through when we learned of the $10,000 price tag.

DISTRIBUTION

Your conspiracy will need to decide how you are going to distribute the food. We have used three ways; the last two save the most money.

• Taking individual orders and buying the items whatever they cost, even if there is no savings on some produce ordered.

• Taking approximately $2 from each member, getting the best buys and dividing the produce evenly.

- Taking a deposit from each member, buying the best buys and then letting each member take what he wants and pay the actual cost. (With this method, it is a good idea to concentrate on foods that will keep for a week in a refrigerator so that if some items are unsold one week, they can be offered again the next week.)

Members will need to take turns doing the following:

- Taking money and orders
- Driving out to get the produce. If your order is over $40 it will probably require two average-sized cars to bring it all back.
- Handling distribution by checking off people who pick up their orders or cashiering individual purchases.

Of course, the best way to get produce is to grow your own. That way you will get the freshest possible food and you will know exactly the kind of care that your plants received while they were growing. If you do this, then "distribution" will be merely a sharing of "extras."

YOUR OWN GARDEN

If you do start your own vegetable garden, seed growers will give you good prices on bulk orders of seeds, roots, etc. We obtained untreated seeds at growers' prices with quick shipment from the W. Atlee Burpee Company, Box L-2001, Clinton, Iowa 52732. If you want to parcel the seeds out into store-size packets, the following equivalents are useful: 1/8 ounce small seeds equals 1 teaspoon (e.g. lettuce, radishes, carrots), 1/2 ounce large seeds equals 1 tablespoon (e.g. peas, beans, corn). A good time to order seeds is in January. You will have a better selection and get prompter shipment.

COMPARATIVE PRODUCE PRICES

Item	Conspiracy Price	Discount Price	Item	Conspiracy Price	Discount Price
Asparagus per lb.	51¢	59¢	Carrots per bunch	14¢	19¢
Bell pepper per lb.	25	26	Parsley per bunch	06	15
Eggplant ea.	24	49	Cabbage per head	21	38
Yellow onions per lb.	13	23	Grapefruit ea.	10	25
Bok choy per bunch	20	40	Bananas per lb.	11	12½
Banana squash per lb.	11	10	Pineapple ea.	41	98
Broccoli per bunch	36	49	Oranges per lb.	13	25
Red leaf lettuce per head	16	25	Hauer apples per lb.	17	35

Produce/How to Eat It

BRENDA'S ANTIPASTO

Put in a 1-1/2-quart jar:
1 green pepper, seeded and
    coarsely chopped
1-1/2 cups cauliflowerets
1-1/2 cups whole or halved
    mushrooms
1-1/2 cups ripe olives
1 to 2 onions, coarsely chopped
Put the following ingredients
into a saucepan and bring to a
boil:
1 cup olive oil
1-1/2 cups wine or cider vinegar
4 tablespoons sugar
3/4 teaspoon pepper
1-1/2 teaspoons salt
1 garlic clove, minced
    or mashed
Remove from heat and allow to
cool 5 minutes. Pour over contents
of jar, screw on lid and place jar
on its side. Marinate for at least
4 days, turning jar once daily.
Makes 5-1/2 cups

GUACAMOLE

With a fork or potato masher,
mash together:
1 avocado, skinned and pitted
1/2 teaspoon salt
1 teaspoon cumin
1 teaspoon garlic powder, or
1 garlic clove, mashed
1 teaspoon minced fresh chili
    pepper
1 tablespoon mayonnaise
2 green onions, chopped
6 cherry tomatoes, quartered
This is good served as a dip with
carrot slices or crackers.
Serves 3 to 4

WHOLE BEET BORSHCH

Place in a 2-quart pot:
1 beet, including tops, chopped
    somewhat small
milk to cover
Cover (preferably with a glass
lid so you can see what is
happening without lifting the lid)
and simmer for about 30 minutes,
or until the beets are easily sliced
with a fork.
Serves 2 to 3

KOREAN KIM-CHI

Soak overnight until wilted in:
1 gallon water, mixed with
1 cup salt
10 Chinese cabbages,
    chopped bite size
Drain brine but don't rinse.
Thoroughly mix in with cabbage
the following spices, using more
if you want to:
4 hot peppers, chopped
5 tablespoons grated ginger root
5 tablespoons minced garlic
Add water just to cover cabbages
and compress with fitted plate.
Have everything in a large urn,
preferably earthen 5-gallon,
cover tightly and bury under-
ground or place in a cellar (even
temperature is more important
than coolness) for approximately
2 weeks. Put mixture into jars
and refrigerate for a minimum of
1 month (longer is better). Eat
only when temptation over-
whelms. This improves for
about 6 months.

CARROT SOUP

In a heavy 3-quart pot, sauté:
3/4 cup chopped onion, in
2 tablespoons butter or oil
Add to pot and simmer for
30 minutes:
3 cups carrots, chopped or run
   through a grinder
4 cups chicken stock or bouillon
2 tablespoons tomato paste
2 tablespoons barley
Purée mixture in blender or run
through a food mill and return
to pot. Add to soup, heat and
serve:
1/2 cup evaporated milk, double-
   strength powdered milk or
   cream
salt and pepper to taste
1 tablespoon butter
Those of you who hate cooked
carrots will still like this soup.
Serves 4 to 5

JELLED CUCUMBER SOUP

Chill:
4 cups strained chicken broth
Remove fat that hardens on the
surface. Bring broth to a boil
and add:
1-1/2 tablespoons unflavored
   gelatin, softened in
1/4 cup cold water
Then add to hot soup:
juice of 1 or 2 lemons
2 to 3 drops green food coloring
   (optional)
salt and cayenne pepper to taste
Let soup cool, place in refrigerator and chill until thick but
not set.
Slice in thin rounds and then
quarter each slice of:
1 medium-sized cucumber,
   peeled, if desired
Stir cucumber pieces into jelling
soup. Return soup to refrigerator
and chill until set. Serve as a side
dish or as a dip for crackers.
Serves 4 to 5

POTATO AND LEEK SOUP

Brown for 10 minutes in the
bottom of a soup pot:
1 bunch leeks, very thinly sliced
3 celery stalks, very thinly sliced
3 tablespoons butter
Add to vegetables, cover and
simmer for 10 minutes:
1 cup water
Add, cover and cook for 10
minutes more:
2-1/2 cups diced potatoes
Add and simmer until potatoes
are tender:
3 cups milk
Add to soup and serve:
salt, pepper and cayenne
   pepper to taste
Serves 4 to 6

SPINACH SOUP

Cook until done:
2 bunches spinach, in
a little water
Drain and squeeze out spinach
juice into the cooking water.
Reserve liquid and chop spinach.
In a medium-sized pot, sauté
until onion is translucent:
1/4 onion, finely chopped
2 tablespoons butter
Sprinkle over onion, cooking
1 minute while stirring with a
wooden spoon (don't allow to
brown):
1 tablespoon flour
Add and cook over medium-low
heat, stirring until thickened:
the reserved spinach liquid
the chopped spinach
Then add and heat:
enough water or chicken stock
   to make 2 to 3 cups liquid
1 cup milk
1 teaspoon salt
pepper, cayenne pepper, nutmeg
   and lemon juice to taste
Ladle into bowls and place on
top of each:
a dab of yogurt
Serves 4

GREEK CABBAGE SOUP

In a big, heavy pot, sauté until
onion is translucent:
1 large onion, chopped
4 tablespoons oil
Add to pot and bring to boil:
2 quarts hot water
2 cups chopped tomatoes
1 to 2 cups cooked, chopped
   lamb breast with excess
   fat removed
2 parsley sprigs, chopped
1 small head cabbage, thinly
   sliced
1 tablespoon brown sugar
2 tablespoons wine vinegar
salt and pepper
Cover and simmer 45 minutes.
Serves 8 to 10

BULGUR WHEAT SALAD

Have ready:
1 cup bulgur wheat
2 cups boiling water
1 tablespoon chicken bouillon
Pour boiling water over bouillon
and bulgur and let stand 2 hours,
until light and puffy.

Mix together to make dressing:
6 tablespoons salad oil
1/4 cup wine vinegar
1/2 teaspoon salt
1/4 teaspoon coarsely ground
   black pepper
Marinate in dressing:
1/4 pound mushrooms, sliced
Add to the bulgur the following
and half of the dressing with
mushrooms removed:
6 radishes, chopped
1 tomato, chopped
4 stuffed olives, thinly sliced
1/4 cup minced green onions
1/2 cup raw green peas
1/3 cup chopped parsley
Spread in salad bowl:
1 head endive, torn in pieces
1 head leaf lettuce, torn in pieces
1/2 pound spinach, torn in pieces
Place bulgur mixture in center
of lettuce and garnish with:
additional peas, chopped tomato
   and radish
the marinated mushrooms
Drizzle remaining dressing on
greens and serve.
Serves 12 generously

GREEK SALAD

Place in salad bowl:
1 head of lettuce, torn in pieces
3 celery stalks, minced
2 tomatoes, minced
2 green onions, minced
1 cucumber, minced
1 green pepper, minced
Mix together, pour over salad
and toss:
1/3 cup olive oil
1/4 cup wine vinegar
1/2 teaspoon oregano
salt and pepper to taste
Arrange on top of salad:
1/2 to 3/4 cup Kalamati olives
8 anchovy fillets
1/2 pound feta cheese, cut in
    wedges
This is tangy and salty.
Serves 6 to 8

ERICA'S MARINATED MUSHROOM SALAD

Combine and coat well with
the oil:
16 mushrooms, sliced
3 to 4 green onions, sliced
3 cups cherry tomatoes,
    green tops removed
1 cucumber, peeled if skin is
    bitter, and thinly sliced
1/2 teaspoon oregano
1/4 teaspoon thyme
1/4 teaspoon marjoram
1/8 teaspoon pepper
1/2 teaspoon sweet basil
1/4 teaspoon seasoned salt
1/3 cup salad oil, or
1/2 cup olive oil
Toss in and marinate at least
4 hours:
1/4 cup tarragon vinegar
Wrap in towel and place in
refrigerator:
1 medium-sized head lettuce,
    washed, drained and torn
    in pieces
Just before serving, mix ingredients together gently.
Serves 4 to 6 generously

GREEN SALAD

Place in a jar, cover, shake vigor-
ously and refrigerate:
2 tablespoons capers
1/4 cup chopped onion
1 garlic clove, crushed
1-1/2 teaspoons prepared mustard
1-1/2 teaspoons pepper
1/2 teaspoon oregano
juice of 1 lime
juice of 1 lemon
1/4 teaspoon salt
1-1/2 cups salad oil
1/2 cup white vinegar
Mix together in a salad bowl:
4 heads assorted greens, torn
    in pieces
1/4 pound blue cheese, crumbled
Shake dressing, pour 1/2 cup of
it over the salad greens and toss.
Serves 12 generously

CALIFORNIA SALAD

Wash, dry, chill and break into
bits:
**greens in the proportion of
2/3 romaine, 1/3 red leaf,
butter lettuce and spinach**
Toss with greens, just to coat:
**approximately 1/4 cup peanut or
other vegetable oil**
Toss in greens any or all of
the following:
celery slices
mushroom slices
thin slices of zucchini
artichoke hearts
alfalfa sprouts
chopped parsley
hearts of palm
Sprinkle on salad:
juice of 1 lemon
garlic salt and oregano to taste
Toss again with:
**approximately 1 cup sunflower
and/or sesame seeds**
Sprinkle well with:
1/2 cup grated Parmesan cheese
Serves 10

ARTICHOKES

Place in pressure cooker or
steamer:
2 to 4 artichokes
water to 1/4-inch depth
1/2 lemon, cut up, or
**1 tablespoon freshly-squeezed
lemon juice**
2 to 3 bay leaves
1 tablespoon oil
1 or 2 garlic cloves, cut in half
salt to taste
Cook about 10 minutes at 15
pounds pressure if using
a pressure cooker, 1 hour if
using a steamer, adding more
water as needed.

FRIED SPINACH

In an oiled skillet or wok, stir
until spinach is tender and
bright green:
1 bunch spinach, torn in pieces
3/4 cup chopped parsley
salt to taste
2 tablespoons sesame seeds
**a little water, adding more as it
evaporates**
1 tablespoon or more soy sauce
good sprinkling of basil
Good served over rice, and if you
have it, with plum sauce or
chutney.
Serves 2

CARROT PAPRIKA TZIMMES

Fry in oil until onions are translucent:
4 carrots, thinly sliced
1 large onion, chopped
6 garlic cloves, minced
Add to vegetables:
**1 cup chicken broth, bouillon
or water**
**2 to 3 tablespoons paprika
(enough to make everything red)**
several dashes cayenne pepper
salt to taste
Cover and simmer until carrots
are tender. Then add, to thicken
liquid:
**1 tablespoon or more whole-
wheat flour**
This goes well with rice,
potatoes or fish.
Serves 4

CARROT RAISIN TZIMMES

Follow preceding recipe omitting
the paprika and cayenne pepper
and substituting:
1 to 1-1/2 cups raisins

23

Produce/How to Eat It

EXTREMELY EDIBLE ZUCCHINI AND RICE

Fry in oil until golden:
1 onion, chopped
4 garlic cloves, minced
1 cup raw brown rice
Add to pan:
1 cup beef or chicken broth
1/2 teaspoon or more ground
   rosemary
1/2 to 3/4 cup chopped parsley
sprinkle of turmeric
salt to taste
Cover and simmer over low heat.
When first cup of broth is
absorbed add:
1 cup broth
Just before rice mixture is
done, fry in oil until it turns
bright green:
1 pound zucchini, sliced in
   rounds
1 or more garlic cloves, chopped
salt and pepper
(Please do not ruin this recipe
by letting the zucchini get yellow
and mushy.)

When the rice is done, add the
zucchini and:
1/2 cup grated Cheddar cheese
Mix in until it melts and then
add:
3/4 cup olives, sliced
Variations: Substitute 1 celery
stalk, chopped, and 1/2 pound
mushrooms, chopped, or 1 eggplant, chopped, for the zucchini.
Serves 4

RED CABBAGE

Put into a pot:
1 red cabbage, shredded
4 tablespoons melted butter
2 medium-sized onions, finely
   chopped
1/2 teaspoon nutmeg
2 teaspoons salt
pepper to taste
2 cups water
2 tablespoons cider vinegar
Stir to mix, cover and cook for
30 minutes. Add to pot and
cook for an additional 30
minutes:
4 firm apples, cored and sliced
3 teaspoons freshly squeezed
   lemon juice
sugar, if the apples aren't sweet
Serves 8

FLORIE'S POCURA

Mix together to make a thin
batter:
1 cup garbanzo flour
pinch salt
pinch baking powder
pinch pepper
1/2 teaspoon cayenne pepper
1/2 teaspoon coriander
approximately 1 cup water
Have ready:
1 onion, thinly sliced
1 bunch spinach, cut in
   1/2-inch strips
boiling oil, for deep frying
Place 2 to 3 tablespoons of the
vegetables in the batter, remove
and drop into the boiling oil. Fry
until brown on both sides. Repeat
with remaining vegetables and
serve immediately. This is also
good made with eggplant and
soaked lima beans.
Serves 4 as a side dish,
2 as a main dish.

Produce/How to Eat It

HUNGARIAN SALAD CHOW MEIN

Sauté in oil until onion is cooked:
2 to 3 medium-sized carrots, grated
1/2 pound mushrooms, sliced
1 large onion, chopped
3/4 cup chopped parsley
1 celery stalk, chopped
6 garlic cloves, minced
Add to vegetables until they are red:
2 to 3 tablespoons paprika
Add and cook 5 minutes:
1 package ramen noodles, cooked
oil, as needed
Then add the following seasonings and as much liquid as desired:
salt and cayenne pepper to taste
approximately 1 cup stock, bouillon or water
Serves 3 to 4

GARBANZABLED ZUCCHINI

Shake:
4 to 5 zucchini, thinly sliced, in wheat flour
Combine, to make a thin batter:
1 cup garbanzo flour
approximately 1 cup water
1 egg, beaten (optional)
1 teaspoon salt (optional)
Dip each slice of zucchini into the batter, thinly coating it, and drop into:
boiling oil, about 1/2 inch deep
Deep fry until lightly browned.
Serves 8 as a side dish,
4 as a main dish

TEMPURA

Mix together to make a rather thick batter:
1 cup whole-wheat or garbanzo flour
1 teaspoon salt
1 cup ice water
1 ice cube (optional)
1 egg
Shake selected vegetables in:
flour
Dip the floured vegetables into the batter and deep fry until slightly browned in:
enough oil for deep frying, heated to 350°

Flip the vegetables when they rise to the surface so they get cooked on both sides.
This recipe is also good for boned chicken, small fish and beef chunks. For small fish, clean them, removing the head and the spine (don't worry about the smaller bones). Sprinkle the cavity of the fish with:
flour
spices and/or chopped parsley or chives
Roll up the fish so the tail sticks up and secure into position with a toothpick. Shake the rolled fish in:
flour
Dip in the batter and deep fry as directed for vegetables.

TEMPURA DIP

Mix together in a saucepan and heat before serving:
1/4 cup white wine
1/4 cup vinegar
1/2 cup soy sauce
freshly grated ginger to taste
1/4 to 1/2 cup water
2 tablespoons brown sugar (optional)

ZUCCHINI CASSEROLE

Sauté in oil:
1/4 to 1/2 pound mushrooms,
    sliced
3 medium-sized zucchini, sliced
1 to 2 yellow onions, sliced
Add to vegetables:
salt, pepper, basil, oregano and
    rosemary to taste
Mix together and add to
vegetable mixture:
1 tablespoon melted butter
1/2 pint sour cream or plain
    yogurt
2 tablespoons lemon juice
1 cup grated sharp Cheddar
    cheese
2 tablespoons chopped chives or
    green onion
2 teaspoons paprika
1 egg
Put everything into a buttered
baking dish or loaf pan. Sprinkle
on top:
1/4 to 1/2 cup grated Cheddar
    or Parmesan cheese
bread crumbs or wheat germ
Bake at 350° until brown and
bubbling, about 30 minutes.
Serves 4

CAULIFLOWER QUICHE

Mash with a fork, gradually
blending in half-and-half:
3 ounces cream cheese
1 cup half-and-half
Add to cheese mixture and then
beat with mixer or wire whisk:
1/2 cup soft bread cubes
1/4 cup shredded Parmesan
    cheese
2 eggs, lightly beaten
Stir into mixture:
1 cup cooked cauliflowerets,
    drained
In a large frying pan, sauté until
lightly browned in:
4 tablespoons butter
1 large onion, finely chopped
1/4 pound mushrooms, sliced
Add to frying pan:
1/2 teaspoon tarragon
1/4 teaspoon each thyme and
    rosemary
Stir onion-mushroom mixture
into cream-cheese mixture and
add:
salt to taste
Pour into pie pan or baking dish
and decorate top with:
1/4 pound mushrooms, sliced
Bake at 400° for 25 minutes, or
until top is lightly browned. Let
stand 10 minutes before cutting
and serving to allow it to set.
Serves 6 to 8

CHICKEN LEG PIE
(no chicken or pie crust
needed)

In a 2-1/2-quart casserole, layer
the following ingredients in
order given, ending with the
grated cheese:
1 pound whole-wheat or soy
    noodles, cooked
a light sprinkling of salt,
    cayenne pepper, cumin and
    sesame seeds
3 medium tomatoes, chopped
1/2 cup chopped parsley
1 bunch spinach, torn in pieces
3/4 pound Swiss cheese, sliced
1/2 to 3/4 pound Cheddar cheese,
    grated
Top the casserole with:
1/4 cup soy grits, wheat germ,
    cornmeal or bread crumbs
salt and spices of choice
Bake 30 minutes in a 350° oven.
Note: For more protein, several
beaten eggs can be mixed in with
the cooked noodles before they
are put into the casserole.
The flavor of this dish reminds
you of chicken.
Serves 3 or 4 with a
salad on the side

Produce/How to Eat It

SPINACH PIE
(Spanakopeta)

Sauté:
2 bunches green onions,
    chopped, in
1/2 cup olive oil
Remove onions and reserve
olive oil.
Combine thoroughly in a bowl
with the onions:
3 pounds spinach, washed,
    dried and chopped
3/4 to 1 cup chopped parsley
1/2 teaspoon sweet basil
1 pound feta cheese, crumbled
8 egg whites, beaten stiff
8 egg yolks, beaten smooth
salt to taste
Have ready:
1/2 pound phyllo dough sheets
    (purchased or strudel dough,
    page 103)
1/2 pound melted butter
the reserved olive oil
Place 1 sheet of phyllo in a
greased 9 x 12-inch baking dish.
Brush sheet with butter and olive
oil. Repeat with four more
sheets. Place the filling on top of
the phyllo and then pile on the
remaining sheets, brushing each
one with butter and/or olive oil.

Bake 45 minutes at 350° until
slightly browned. Remove from
oven, let cool until it can be
handled, turn over and return to
baking dish to brown other side.
When done, cut the spinach pie
into squares and serve. Note:
This filling can also be used for
strudel, or it can be made into
many individual pies.

SANDI'S VEGEBURGERS

Mix together:
1/4 pound mushrooms, finely
    chopped
1 green onion, finely chopped
Add to the mixture:
salt, pepper and oregano (or any
    other herbs you like) to taste
Stir in:
2 eggs, beaten
Then add, being careful not to
make a mush:
1/2 cup bread crumbs
3/4 cup (1/4 pound) grated
    Cheddar cheese
Form into 4 patties and fry in oil
over low heat. They should be
crisp on the outside and moist on
the inside when done. For additional flavor, add chopped onions
and garlic to the pan when
cooking the burgers.
Serves 2

HAPPY VEGIES

Boil in very little water:
2 small carrots, finely chopped
1 pound peas, shelled
1 pound green beans, finely
    chopped
2 potatoes or squash, finely
    chopped
1/2 teaspoon turmeric
Meanwhile, in a blender jar
purée until smooth:
1/3 of a green chili
1/2 cup shredded coconut
    (preferably fresh)
1/4 to 1/3 cup cumin seeds
1/2 teaspoon salt
1/4 pound sweet butter, melted
    and skimmed, or
1/4 cup coconut oil
water, as needed
Mix boiled vegetables with contents of blender jar and serve.
Serves 4

BAKED ORANGE CARROT RING

Grate fine:
1 pound carrots, washed and
  scraped
Beat together with carrots:
3 eggs
1/2 cup flour
Stir in and mix well:
1-1/2 cups orange juice
1-1/2 teaspoons salt
1/4 teaspoon Tabasco sauce
1 tablespoon melted butter
1 small onion, minced
Pour into a buttered 5-cup ring
mold and bake at 375° for 1 hour,
or until golden on top. Let stand
5 minutes and turn out on serving platter. Fill center of ring
with:
1 or more oranges, peeled and
  sliced
1 cup peas, shelled and cooked
  or left raw
1 cup sliced mushrooms, sautéed
Serves 8

GREEN TOMATO MINCEMEAT

Put through a food grinder:
3 pounds green tomatoes, cored
Measure tomatoes and add:
equal amount of water
Place in pot, bring to boil and
simmer 30 minutes. While tomatoes are cooking, put through
food grinder:
3 pounds tart apples, peeled,
  cored and chopped
2 pounds seed-free raisins
When tomatoes have finished
simmering, drain well and add:
the ground apples and raisins
8 cups brown sugar
2 tablespoons salt
1/2 pound suet or butter
1 cup vinegar
2 tablespoons cinnamon
1 teaspoon ground cloves
1 teaspoon ground nutmeg
1/2 pound candied lemon and
  orange peels (page 119)
1/4 cup freshly-squeeezed lemon
  juice
Cook slowly until thick. Seal in
canning jars or pressure can at
10 pounds for 10 minutes.
Makes approximately 4 quarts

SWEET POTATO BISCUITS

Mix together:
1 small sweet potato, steamed
  and mashed (about 3/4 cup)
2/3 cup milk
4 tablespoons melted butter
  or oil
1-1/4 cups whole-wheat flour
1 tablespoon baking powder
1 tablespoon honey
1/2 teaspoon salt
Turn out on floured cloth or
board. Knead lightly, and when
it looks smooth, roll out and cut
out biscuits. Bake at 450° for
about 15 minutes. Serve hot
with butter.
Makes approximately 12 biscuits

Produce/How to Eat It

PERSIMMON PUDDING

Mix together:
2 cups brown sugar
2-1/2 cups whole-wheat flour
2 teaspoons baking soda
3 teaspoons baking powder
1/2 teaspoon each cinnamon,
  nutmeg and salt
2 cups persimmon pulp
1/2 cup milk, soured with
  lemon juice
3 teaspoons oil
2 teaspoons vanilla
1-1/2 cups chopped walnuts
  or pecans
1-1/2 cups golden raisins
Put in a greased baking dish or
mold and bake at 325° for 1 hour.
Serves 6 to 8

PUMPKIN CHEESE PIE

Prepare prebaked pie crust on
page 89 and use half of dough.
Beat together until smooth:
6 ounces cream cheese
3/4 cup sugar
2 teaspoons cinnamon
1 teaspoon ground ginger
1/4 teaspoon ground cloves
Blend into cream cheese mixture:
2 eggs, beaten
Then add, mixing thoroughly:
2 cups cooked pumpkin, mashed
Pour filling into pie shell and
bake at 325° for 35 minutes, or
until center no longer looks
liquid when pan is shaken
slightly. Remove from oven.
To make topping, mix together:
1/2 pint sour cream
6 tablespoons sugar
1 teaspoon vanilla extract
Spread topping on pie and
decorate with:
1/2 cup pecan halves (optional)
Return pie to 325° oven for
10 minutes. Remove and let cool.
Serves 8

GRANDMA MORRIS' THANKSGIVING PUDDING

Cream together:
1/2 pound figs, chopped
1/2 cup suet, chopped
Soak:
2-1/2 cups bread crumbs, in
1 cup milk
To the suet-fig mixture add:
3 eggs, well beaten
1 cup brown sugar
1 teaspoon salt
2 teaspoons baking powder
3/4 teaspoon cinnamon
1/2 teaspoon nutmeg
Dredge in flour and add to
suet mixture:
1/2 pound seeded raisins
1/2 cup chopped walnuts
2 tablespoons flour
Then add:
the soaked bread crumbs
and more milk if necessary
  to moisten
Place in buttered pudding mold
and steam for 3 hours.
Serve with hard sauce.
Serves 16

Cheese and Milk

In the United States, most cheeses are made from pasteurized milk. Many have dyes in them and some have stabilizers. A grocery store manager is more interested in the shelf life of his stock than in your longevity or health. You can get natural cheese, however, if you look around for sources. Since a conspiracy can save its members 30 to 40 percent on the cost of cheese and since most cheese has a protein value equal to beef, buying it is well worth the effort. Cheeses made without stabilizers may mold more quickly and those made without dyes may look funny, but they do taste better and are better for you than the processed variety. Also, most cheeses can be cut into chunks, wrapped and frozen (except Cheddar) to prevent molding if you buy more than can be eaten in a week or two.

GETTING ORGANIZED

First choose a member to call around the local dairies and cheese specialty shops. (You'll find them listed in the yellow pages under "dairy" and "cheese.") The caller should:

- Explain what your conspiracy is doing.
- Ask for prices on your conspirators' favorite cheeses.
- Ask for a printed price list of the business's entire stock.
- Ask if the business will deliver the cheeses, and if so, is there a fee for the service.
- Find out how big the blocks of each cheese are and if the business will sell you parts of them.
- Ask if there is a discount for paying in cash.

After you have all this information, choose one supplier. This one may not be the cheapest of those who were willing to sell to you, but the lowest prices in the world aren't worth dealing with unpleasant people every week.

GETTING THE CHEESE

Once you have decided on a supplier and which cheeses you are going to list, post this information where all the members will see it. Conspirators should now sign up to be cheese coordinators. You should also decide how long the cheese coordinatorship should last: a week? a month? The coordinator will:

- Take orders and money from each conspirator.
- Add up the amounts of each cheese ordered and decide how many blocks or wheels of each variety to order. A kitty makes ordering easier; the extra money will enable you to buy a six-pound block of cheese when only four pounds have been prepaid. Without a kitty you could only buy this cheese if you bought less than the ordered amount of another type. After all, if you have only $60 prepaid for cheese, you can't buy $61 of cheese. Before buying more than ordered, it is a good idea to find out whether your fellow conspirators are impulse buyers, who will buy the extras, or if they will accept credits toward future orders in place of an immediate refund.
- Make sure someone picks up the cheese, or is home to receive it if it is to be delivered. Be sure he has a large enough refrigerator to store it, also.
- Make sure there are people to cut the cheese.

Try to imagine yourself in a room with 80 pounds of cheese, some of which is yours, and your only weapons are a knife or wire, a scale and a ruler. Cutting cheese is a rewarding job; cutters can nibble the inevitable crumbs. Nibbling, of course, is the best way to find out what an unusual cheese tastes like. If you like it you can add some extra to your order, and if you don't, it won't sit there growing mold in your refrigerator. By the way, cheese doesn't come with dotted lines marking off each pound. The closest approximation to cutting even pounds that we have found is to try to whack off 1/6 of a 6-pound block. A ruler helps. Procedure involves:

CUTTING THE CHEESE

- Making a master list for each cheese showing who is getting some and how much he is getting.
- Washing your hands and tying back your hair.
- Picking up a block of cheese and finding the appropriate master list. Look at the list to see what size chunks you should try to cut; for example, there might be orders for one 2-pound piece and four 1-pound pieces.
- Cutting up the entire block.
- Weighing each piece. After weighing, write down on a small piece of paper the name of the cheese and its weight. (All cheeses look alike . . .)
- Wrapping the cheese in plastic to keep it from drying out. (Yes, plastic; wax wrap won't do.) The easiest way to wrap large chunks is to put them in grocery-store produce bags (most grocers will sell you these at 1/2 cent each or you can buy them wholesale). You can use plastic wrap or sandwich bags to wrap the smaller pieces; that will cost about 1/4 cent per piece. You can charge an extra penny per item to cover these costs.

- Putting the cheese into large paper bags that each conspirator has provided for this purpose. Each bag has its owner's name on it, the cheeses he has ordered and the amount he has paid.
- Writing onto the bag the wrapping charges and any difference in the cost of the cheese received from that ordered. An easy way to do this is to use the chart below. Depending on your scale and your patience you can calculate prices to the nearest 1/4 ounce or let the cheese go if it is within 2 ounces of the ordered amount. Write the difference between the amount that was paid and the amount that is owed, with a plus or minus sign, in large figures on the cheese bag of each conspirator.
- Taking the cheese to the distribution location. If it arrives before the distribution time, place the soft cheese like ricotta and cream cheese in a refrigerator. Be sure you put names on each cheese so the proper owner can find it. If there is any extra cheese, put it in a refrigerator too. Make sure it is labeled with its name and weight.
- Distributing and cashiering the cheese.

If you want lower prices still, and your cheese business gets over $100 a week or you decide to join with some other conspiracies in your area, you can look in the yellow pages under "cheese—wholesale" and set up accounts with the people who have been selling to your supplier. Don't mention that you have been buying your cheese elsewhere or for that matter that you have been buying cheese at all. Wholesalers hate to see their current customers lose business, even though their own business will stay the same. If it's a multi-conspiracy project, you will probably need a double-level cheese cutting. At the first level you will cut the cheese into the amounts ordered by each conspiracy; at the second you will cut the cheese into the amounts ordered by individuals.

CHEESE PRICES PER OUNCE

oz.	75¢	80¢	85¢	90¢	95¢	$1.00	$1.05	$1.10	$1.15	$1.20	$1.40
1/4	1	1	1	1	1	2	2	2	2	2	2
1/2	2	3	3	3	3	3	3	3	4	4	4
3/4	4	4	4	4	4	5	5	5	5	6	6
1	5	5	5	6	6	6	7	7	7	8	9
2	9	10	11	11	12	13	13	14	14	15	18
3	14	15	16	17	18	19	20	21	22	23	26
4	19	20	21	23	24	25	26	27	29	30	35
5	23	25	27	28	30	31	33	34	36	38	44
6	28	30	32	34	36	38	39	41	43	45	53
7	33	35	37	40	42	44	46	48	50	53	61
8	38	40	43	45	48	50	53	55	58	60	70
9	42	45	48	51	53	56	59	62	65	68	79
10	47	50	53	56	59	63	66	69	72	75	88
11	52	55	58	62	65	69	72	76	79	83	96
12	56	60	63	68	71	75	79	83	86	90	1.05
13	61	65	69	73	77	81	85	90	93	98	1.14
14	66	70	74	79	83	88	92	96	1.01	1.05	1.23
15	70	75	80	84	89	94	98	1.03	1.08	1.13	1.31

Case out your local dairymen the same way you did the cheese suppliers. In addition:

MILK

- Ask if the milk is available in glass bottles or paper cartons.
- Find out about by-products and brand names. (Is brand B whipping cream thicker than brand A? Whose butter tastes better? Whose cottage cheese?)
- Pay special attention to small dairies. They are more likely to sell you a replacement bottle if you break one or to let you return milk if you overordered by mistake.
- Ask about specialty milks. Our pasteurized milk dairy sells "cream on top," unhomogenized milk and our raw milk dairy has both cow and goat milk, and real chocolate milk, not chocolate drink like most dairies sell.
- Ask if the dairy will deliver. This is especially nice in states like California where milk is "fair traded" and the dairy can't give you a discount for picking it up yourself. (See next page for a list of "fair traded" states.)
- Ask about the discount schedule. Whether or not your milk is "fair traded," your dairy will have lower prices for purchases of greater volumes.
- Ask if you will need any permits. The requirements vary from city to city.

In states where the price of milk is not regulated, you can sell the milk cheaply at your weekly distribution. Where prices are controlled, you must sell the milk at the price set by the state. Your conspiracy can save up the difference between what you paid for the milk and what you must charge for it and give monthly patronage refunds. You could save a percentage of the money to buy a refrigerator or other needed items. (Used refrigerators with small freezer compartments sell for $10 to $20; sometimes you can get one free.)

Under refrigeration fresh milk keeps for at least 10 days, unopened, so your conspiracy can buy for a whole week ahead. Your milk will be bottled at the dairy the morning of delivery rather than sitting several days at a store. Milk that won't fit into members' home refrigerators can be stored in the conspiracy refrigerator; it is a good idea to write members' names onto their cartons to prevent mixups. Since the conspiracy refrigerator will get less use than a home refrigerator, do not set the temperature as cold. Forty degrees is good.

It is best not to get grand ideas about buying your milk in bulk and packaging it yourself. Even if your local health department did not shut you down, it still would not be sanitary. And, in most states the only way to buy milk cheaply in bulk is to buy a whole tank car full. Even the five- or six-gallon containers are not economical; they actually sell for more per unit than packaged milk. Generally it is only restaurants that buy milk in this size container and they are paying for the convenience of not having to worry about a lot of little containers. Remember you are in a food conspiracy in order to get the best quality food possible at the cheapest possible prices. Packaging as fussy a food as milk yourself is a step in the wrong direction.

If the conspiracies in your area are buying more than $500 worth of milk each week, you might consider setting up a milk distributorship cooperative. A distributor gets a lower price from the dairy than stores or conspiracies can get. The profits—after buying a truck, licensing, insuring, feeding and repairing it—can go back to the conspiracies.

DISTRIBUTING MILK

With milk you will need a markup. One reason for this is that milk is sold at strange prices like 54.57 cents per gallon, less a 16 percent discount if purchased in a volume of at least $175 or 15 percent discount for a volume of $125. You can't charge someone *that* for a half gallon of milk. You will need to charge 63 or 64 cents, maybe more if you tend to break bottles.

You will need weekly milk coordinators; that is, each week a different member will coordinate the ordering and distribution. When all the members, including new ones, have done this job once, the rotation should start over, but not before then. It will be the coordinator's job:

• To add up orders and phone them in to the dairy.
• To take money and orders for the following week's milk, and turn them over to the next week's coordinator.
• To make sure that each member gets what he paid for.
• To make sure the dairy gets paid.
• If you get a distributorship, make sure that there is a driver for the truck.

Milk rots quickly so mistakes must be caught quickly. You might find 20 half gallons of low-fat milk in glass bottles that nobody wants sitting in your back yard. Be sure you double check your adding at every step or you will end up in the hole. This cannot be stressed too much. It is very important that everything be paid for in advance. If your dairy charges deposits on glass bottles, your members should pay deposits on glass bottles.

MILK PRICE CONTROLS The following states have controls for both wholesale and retail prices: Alabama, California, Louisiana, Maine, Montana, Nevada, New Jersey, North Dakota, Pennsylvania, South Carolina, South Dakota, Vermont, Virginia, Puerto Rico. Wyoming has controls on wholesale prices only. Massachusetts and North Carolina have the authority to control prices but are not using it. The other states do not have controls. This information is based on the USDA report "Dairy Situation," 1971.

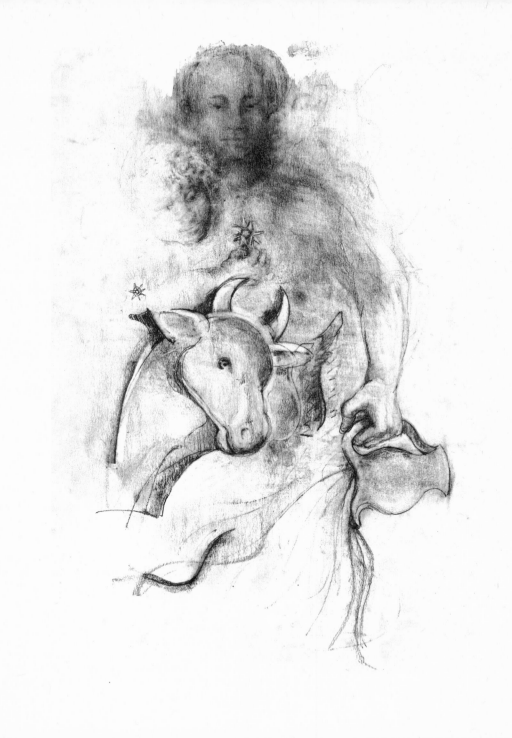

Cheese and Milk/How to Eat It

CHEESE AND SPUD SOUP

Combine in a soup pot:
2 tablespoons flour
1 tablespoon butter or oil
Heat very gradually and
add to flour mixture:
1 cup milk
Simmer gently until it thickens.
Add and mix well, then bring to
boil:
1-1/2 cups diced unpeeled pota-
    toes that have been simmered
    in milk 20 minutes, or 1-1/2
    cups leftover unpeeled mashed
    potatoes
salt and pepper to taste
Add and stir until melted:
1 cup or more grated sharp
    Cheddar cheese
Suggested additions: paprika,
cayenne, dill, leftover cooked
fish, celery, Parmesan cheese,
toasted bread, sesame seeds,
any leftover vegetables.

CHEESE SOUP

Fry in bottom of soup pot until
soft but not browned:
1 to 2 tablespoons finely chopped
    onion, in
1 tablespoon butter or oil
Add to pot and bring to boil:
1-1/4 cups hot water
2 tablespoons flour, mixed with
    a little milk
2-1/2 cups milk
Add to pot and simmer until
soup thickens:
salt, cayenne pepper and thyme
    to taste
Just before serving add to pot
and stir in:
2 to 4 tablespoons grated cheese
    (more for a thicker soup)

DESMID'S COTTAGE CHEESE FLOWER SALAD

For each serving, have ready:
1 scoop cottage cheese
1/2 banana, sliced in rounds
1/2 cup raisins
Place cottage cheese in center of
medium-sized plate. Arrange
banana slices symmetrically
around cottage cheese and place
a raisin in the center of each
banana slice.

MORAGA HILL PARMESAN SALAD DRESSING

Mix into salad:
1/2 cup oil
Then add and stir in:
1 cup red wine vinegar
Sprinkle on top of salad and
then stir in:
1/2 teaspoon salt
1/2 teaspoon chopped garlic
pepper and basil to taste
1/2 to 1 cup grated Parmesan
    cheese
This is especially good in a green
salad that includes raisins and
celery.
Makes 1-1/2 cups, or dressing
for a salad for 8

COTTAGE QUEAZE

In a 1- to 1-1/2-quart casserole
or 4 custard cups, heat
in a 200° to 250° oven:
1 pint cottage cheese
Meanwhile, sauté in:
oil or butter
1/2 onion, chopped
1 cup chopped mushrooms
1 stalk celery, chopped, or
1/2 cup water chestnuts, sliced
any leftover meat, cut in cubes, or
1 cup sunflower seeds or nuts
Spoon over cottage cheese
and serve.
Serves 2 to 3

TURKISH YOGURT

Mix together:
1/2 pint yogurt
1/4 to 1/3 cup milk
1 garlic clove, minced
1/2 cucumber, thinly sliced or
shredded
Eat plain or pour over vegetables,
salads or cooked grains.
Serves 4 as a dressing,
or 1 if eaten plain.

YOGURT
(From Canned Milk)

Blend together in a large container, adding each ingredient in
order given:
1 13-1/2-ounce can evaporated
milk
2 cups hot water
1 cup non-instant powdered milk
3 tablespoons yogurt
2 cups warm water
Pour into leftover plastic cartons,
such as cottage cheese comes in,
and place in a pan of hot water.
When the water cools, pour it out
and add fresh hot water. Do not
use boiling water. Yogurt will set
in 3 to 5 hours. Refrigerate. When
cool, crush or slice fresh strawberries or other fresh fruit or froz-
en unsweetened fruit and pour
yogurt over the fruit. This mixture can be frozen for popsicles.
Makes 1 quart

YOGURT
(From Powdered Milk)

Mix together well (a blender
helps):
1 cup instant powdered milk, or
1/2 cup non-instant powdered
milk
3-1/2 cups warm water

Blend in thoroughly:
1 tablespoon prepared yogurt
1 tablespoon vanilla extract
(optional)
1 tablespoon honey (optional)
Pour mixture into clean 1-pint
jars. Screw on jar lids. Place jars
on a heating pad set at 110°.
(This will be either "medium" or
"high" depending on the pad.)
Put a cardboard box over the
jars and check them after 4 hours.
Depending on the weather and
various other factors, your yogurt
may take up to 8 hours. The
yogurt will be milder if you
refrigerate it before it is completely done. You can put it in
the refrigerator at any stage of
culture growth and take it out
to heat again at your convenience
without affecting the final yogurt.
Makes 1 quart

Another way to make this which
uses less energy is to put the
yogurt mixture into an oven
which has been heated for
5 minutes. Check the oven after
2 or 3 hours by opening the
door a crack to stick your hand
in. Heat the oven for another
minute if necessary. The yogurt
will be done in 3 to 5 hours.

HEALTH-NUT PIZZA

To Make Crust:
Soften:
1 tablespoon active dry yeast, in
1-1/3 cups stock or water
Add:
2 tablespoons olive oil
1 teaspoon sea salt
pinch vegetable broth powder
   (optional)
Add to yeast mixture:
1/2 cup soy flour
2 to 4 tablespoons brewer's yeast
1/4 cup wheat germ (optional)
Add to mixture to make dough:
approximately 3-1/2 cups
   whole-wheat flour
Add to dough:
rosemary, oregano, marjoram,
   etc. (whatever herbs you like)
Knead very well, cover and let
rise in a warm place about
2 hours, or until double in bulk.

To Make Sauce:
Sauté until soft:
1 yellow onion, chopped
1 garlic clove, minced
2 tablespoons olive oil
Whirl in blender and add to
onions, cooking until thick:
1 28-ounce can tomatoes, or
6 fresh tomatoes, boiled
basil, oregano and salt to taste
Add to sauce, if desired:
dash cayenne pepper
more salt
sliced mushrooms and green
   pepper
Knead the dough and roll out
2 crusts. Prick the crusts in
several places and bake at 350°
5 minutes. Have ready:
1 pound mozzarella, Monterey
   Jack or Cheddar cheese, grated
grated Parmesan cheese (optional)
Arrange a layer of the cheese in
each of the crusts, pour on the
sauce and bake at 350° 25 minutes. Put remaining cheese on
the pizzas and return to the oven
for an additional 5 minutes
and serve.
Serves 6 to 8

HELLZAPOPPIN

In a heavy pot bring to a boil
then simmer until rice is done:
1 cup brown rice
2 cups water
1 bunch spinach, chopped
Beat until light and add to cooked
rice and spinach:
4 eggs
Add to rice mixture:
2 tablespoons minced onion
2 tablespoons Tamari soy sauce
2 tablespoons salt
1 pound sharp Cheddar cheese,
   grated
pinch each thyme and marjoram
1 cup milk
Put in a buttered casserole. Pour
over rice mixture:
4 tablespoons melted butter
Bake at 375° for 35 minutes.
Serves 4

RINK'S CHEESE LUNCH

Fry until soft but not brown:
1 small onion, finely chopped, in
1 tablespoon oil
Add to pan and heat thoroughly:
2 tomatoes, chopped
salt and pepper to taste
Add, stirring constantly until melted:
1/2 pound Cheddar cheese, grated
Add slowly while continuing to stir:
1 egg, beaten
Cook 1 minute. Serve in bowls over toast or rice.
Serves 4

CHEESE AND OLIVE NO-BAKE CASSEROLE

Bring to boil in a heavy pot:
1 cup brown rice
2 cups water
Cover and cook over low heat until rice is done, about 40 minutes. Mix into rice:
1 cup chopped ripe olives
salt and pepper to taste
rosemary, oregano, marjoram and parsley
Mix into rice until it melts:
1-1/2 cups grated Cheddar cheese
Serves 4

ONION PIE

To Make Pastry:
Combine, adding just enough ice water so you can handle the dough:
1 cup cornmeal
1 cup whole-wheat or rye flour
1/2 teaspoon sea salt
1/4 cup crude safflower oil
ice water
Roll out and pat into 2 9-inch oiled pie pans. Chill while making filling.

To Make Filling:
Sauté:
3 sliced onions, in
3 tablespoons butter
Place onions in pie shells. Cover with:
1-1/2 cups grated Cheddar cheese
Combine:
1 cup scalded milk, cooled to lukewarm
1/4 cup non-instant powdered milk
3 eggs, beaten
1/2 teaspoon sea salt
1/4 teaspoon thyme
3 tablespoons nutritional yeast

Pour over cheese. Bake at 350° about 30 minutes, or until knife inserted in center comes out clean. Good served hot or cold. It is good reheated.
Serves 8

SWISS CHEESE PIE (Main Dish)

Prepare pie crust on page 89 and use half of dough.
Mix together well and place in pie shell:
1/2 pound Swiss cheese, grated
1/4 to 1/2 cup chopped green onions
1 tablespoon flour
salt and pepper to taste
Mix together and pour over other ingredients:
1/4 cup milk
4 eggs, beaten
Sprinkle on top:
1/4 to 1/3 cup minced parsley
1/2 teaspoon paprika
Bake 10 minutes at 400°. Lower oven temperature to 350° and bake 20 minutes.
Serves 3 to 4

HIGH-PROTEIN CHEESE SOUFFLÉ

Layer in an oiled baking dish, starting with the bread:
4 to 6 slices bread
3 cups grated cheese
Beat together and pour over bread and cheese:
2 cups milk, or
1-1/2 cups milk and
    1/2 cup white wine
3 eggs, beaten
1/2 teaspoon salt
1/2 teaspoon Worcestershire
    sauce
1/2 teaspoon thyme
1/2 teaspoon dry mustard
pepper to taste
Let stand for 30 minutes. Bake at 350° for 1 hour in a pan of hot water, 1 inch deep.
Serves 6

RICOTTA PANCAKES

Beat together until well blended:
1/2 teaspoon salt
4 egg yolks
1 tablespoon vegetable oil
Add and beat in:
1/2 teaspoon baking powder
1 tablespoon whole-wheat flour
2 to 3 ounces ricotta cheese
Beat until stiff and fold into batter:
4 egg whites
Cook pancakes in a hot oiled skillet over medium heat. Flip to brown both sides.
Serves 4

FONDUE

Heat in a heavy 2-quart pot until it starts to bubble:
1 cup white wine
Over low heat, add and stir until thick:
1 pound Monterey Jack or
    Gruyère cheese, grated
2 tablespoons whole-wheat flour
1 tablespoon butter
1 tablespoon Worcestershire or
    soy sauce
This makes a very thick fondue. It is good served with celery chunks for dipping.
Serves 3 to 4

MACARONI WITH CHEESE

Bring to boil:
4 cups salted water
Add:
1 cup macaroni
Cook until macaroni breaks easily when pushed against the side of the pot with a spoon. Drain and place in a buttered 2-quart casserole. Spread around in the macaroni, burying them:
2 chopped green onions, with tops
1 teaspoon chopped chives
6 large mushrooms, sliced
1 pound longhorn cheese, cut
    in strips
Pour on macaroni until it starts to show:
approximately 2 cups milk
Crumble on top:
24 salted crackers
Place on top of crackers:
5 thin pats butter
Bake in a 375° oven 45 to 60 minutes, or until milk solidifies.
Serves 6

PASKA

Following are two recipes for paska, the traditional Russian Easter cheese. It can be eaten alone or with kulich, Russian Easter bread (page 93).

MR. PETROFF'S PASKA

Mix together thoroughly and freeze:
8 pounds dry, unsalted cottage cheese (farmer's or baker's cheese)
4 pounds sweet butter, softened
8 whole eggs, or
5 egg yolks plus 3 whole eggs
1/2 cup slivered almonds
4 vanilla beans, thinly sliced
1 to 2 cups whipping cream
5 to 6 cups sugar
The cheese may be run through a strainer before it is combined with the other ingredients. If there is extra liquid, drain it off before freezing.

SIROVA PASKA

Let soften at room temperature:
4 pounds cream cheese
1/2 pound sweet butter
1 pint sour cream
Thoroughly combine the above ingredients with:
1/2 pint whipping cream
lemon, vanilla or almond extract to taste
When the mixture is mashed together well, place it in the freezer.

CAROB DRINK

Have ready:
1 cup milk
Mix together thoroughly and stir into milk:
1 teaspoon carob powder
1 teaspoon brown sugar or honey
2 tablespoons milk
Serves 1

BUTTERMILK COOLER

Mix in blender:
1 quart buttermilk
juice of 2 oranges
2 tablespoons honey
Serves 4 to 6

REAL STRAWBERRY ICE CREAM

Combine in a 6-quart pot:
1 quart whipping cream
1 quart milk
2 to 3 cups honey
3 to 6 eggs, slightly beaten with
1/3 cup whole-wheat flour
1 to 2 tablespoons gelatin, softened in
1/3 cup water
Stir over low heat until slightly thickened, indicating that the eggs have cooked. Purée and add to above mixture:
3 to 4 baskets (3/4 pound) fresh strawberries
Pour into the can of a 4-quart ice-cream freezer. Freeze, using the ratio of 1 cup salt to 2 quarts ice. The smaller the ice chips, the finer the texture of your ice cream.
Makes 4 quarts

PUDDING FROM SCRATCH

In a 2-quart pot, mix together
well:
6 tablespoons cornstarch, or
4-1/2 tablespoons arrowroot, or
6 tablespoons tapioca flour, or
1/2 cup tapioca pearls, soaked
    1 hour in water
1/2 teaspoon or less salt
1/4 cup brown sugar
6 tablespoons cocoa powder plus
    1/4 cup sugar or 1 vanilla
    bean (optional)
Stir into above powders:
1/4 cup milk
Add and mix thoroughly:
3-1/2 cups milk
Over medium-low heat, stir constantly until thick and bubbles
start to appear. Pour into bowls
and cool before serving.
Serves 4 to 6

DIVINE BREAD PUDDING

Combine thoroughly:
1/3 cup sifted fine bread crumbs
1/8 teaspoon salt
1-1/2 cups milk, scalded
3 tablespoons raisins
1/2 cup sugar
3 eggs, slightly beaten
2 teaspoons butter
Pour into small buttered molds.
Set the molds in a baking dish
containing hot water 1 inch
deep. Bake at 350° for about
40 minutes. Serve with cold
milk or lemon sauce.
Serves 8

MEXICAN HONEY CUSTARD

Stir together in a 2-quart bowl:
1/3 cup honey
2 teaspoons vanilla extract
Add and beat lightly:
7 eggs
dash each nutmeg and cinnamon
Stir in:
1/2 cup cold milk
Gradually add:
4 cups hot milk
Pour in custard cups and place
in a pan of hot water, 1 inch
deep. Bake at 350 ° for about
1 hour.
Serves 8

CHINESE ALMOND DESSERT

Soak for at least 30 minutes:
2 sticks (1/2 ounce) agar agar
    (white kanten), rinsed
    in 2 cups water
Shred up the agar agar
in the liquid and boil it until
dissolved. Stir into
dissolved agar agar:
1 tablespoon brown sugar or
    honey
2 cups milk
1 teaspoon almond extract
Pour in a shallow flat-bottomed
pan approximately 7x11 inches.
Refrigerate for at least 1-1/2
hours, or until solidly jelled. Slice
diagonally at 1/2-inch intervals
to make rhombs or diamonds.
Serve in cups with:
sliced canned or cooked peaches
pouring canning syrup or
sweetened peach cooking water
over top.
Serves 6

Cheese and Milk/How to Eat It

FEROCIOUS CHEESE CAKE

Prepare pie crust on page 89 and use half of dough.
2-1/2 pounds cream cheese, softened
Mix together and add slowly to cheese:
1 cup brown sugar
3/4 cup instant powdered milk
1/4 teaspoon salt
1 teaspoon vanilla extract
1 teaspoon grated lemon rind or anise
Add, one at a time, beating after each addition:
4 eggs plus 2 yolks, or
5 whole eggs
Stir in:
1/4 cup whipping cream
Pour into 9-inch spring-form pan lined with pie crust. Bake 10 minutes at 500°. Lower oven temperature to 200° for 1 hour, cool to room temperature and refrigerate.
Serves 8

SOUR CREAM CAKE

Blend together and pour into buttered 8-inch square or 2 8-inch round pans:
1/2 pint sour cream
2 eggs, or
4 egg yolks
2 cups whole-wheat flour
1 cup brown sugar
1 teaspoon baking soda
pinch salt
2 tablespoons sherry, rum or cherry heering
Bake at 425° 10 to 15 minutes, or until golden and knife inserted in center comes out clean.
Serves 10

SOUR CREAM JOY BALLS

Blend together in a 2-quart bowl:
2/3 cup carob powder
1/2 cup sour cream
1/2 cup honey
1 teaspoon vanilla extract
2 tablespoons toasted soy powder
1 cup or more powdered milk to thicken
1/2 cup each flaked coconut and chopped walnuts
Shape into balls the size of a quarter. Chill before serving.
Makes 24

THE REAL SOUR CREAM AND RAISIN PIE

Prepare pie crust on page 89 and use half of dough.
Beat together until light:
2 eggs, slightly beaten
1 cup sugar, or
3/4 cup honey
Whip into above mixture:
1/2 pint sour cream
Add and mix well:
1 cup raisins, chopped
1/4 to 1/2 teaspoon nutmeg
1/8 teaspoon salt
1 tablespoon lemon juice
Pour mixture into a 9-inch pie pan which has been lined with pastry crust. Bake for 10 minutes at 450°. Lower oven to 350° and bake for 20 minutes.
Makes 1 9-inch pie or serves 8

Eggs and Chickens

EGGS   Now that you have a food conspiracy, you don't want to settle for commercial eggs from mistreated chickens who spend their lives in isolated little coops indoors—chickens that are injected with chemicals, doped up on amphetamines to speed up egg production and lay eggs with thin shells. Now you can have eggs like the health food stores carry. So make a trip to a nearby natural foods store and jot down the address of their supplier of eggs from organically raised chickens. (The name is usually on the carton; if it isn't, just ask an employee.) Then send some members out to the farm to:

- Look around; see if you like how it's run.
- Talk to the farmer and the workmen; do they like their work? Are they well paid?
- Ask if they will sell to you and if they deliver.
- Ask what they feed the chickens and how they treat them for fleas, to see if they're using chemicals as opposed to non-chemical control methods.
- Ask the price of the eggs and if you could get a discount for picking them up yourself. (The price should be 20 to 30 cents less than the health-food store price.)
- Ask if the farmer will give you a discount for returning your egg cartons for reuse. (New cartons cost 5 cents each.)
- Ask if the farmer will sell you some of the chickens that lay these eggs. These organically fed chickens, like the eggs, taste much better than the kind you are used to, so they are really worth all this extra effort. Since some chickens are bred for egg laying, others for eating and others for both, you may need to find a separate supplier for chickens.
- Check to see if the eggs are fertile or sterile, depending on your taste. A fertile egg has a little white spot on it that measures over 1/8 inch. A sterile egg's spot measures less than 1/8 inch. By law, half the eggs in a carton labeled "fertile" must be fertile. While, of course, none of those labeled "sterile" may be fertile.
- While you're there, ask if you may have some droppings for your gardens.

If the farmer refuses to sell to you, ask the local health food stores, one at a time, if they will sell the eggs and chickens to your group at a minimum markup like 5 cents per dozen or per chicken if you promise to pick up your order promptly every week as it is delivered. At least one store in your area should be pleased to have the extra business.

If you are willing to accept commercially raised chickens, make the same offer to a local grocery store—chain stores can probably offer you the best price. In most areas there are no savings available on eggs because they are frequently "loss leaders." (By the way, buy locally grown chickens. They are fresher and therefore taste better than those shipped from out of state.)

If there are no organic eggs in your area, or if even at wholesale you can't afford them, look up "eggs—wholesale" in your yellow pages. You can get a discount on regular (grade A) eggs from these wholesalers, but there are better deals to be had on "chex" and grade B eggs in flats of 2½ dozen. "Chex" eggs are different from regular eggs in that they have hairline cracks in the outer shell but the inner membrane is still intact. These eggs must be handled more delicately than grade A eggs and therefore are not suitable for normal merchandising. Also, these eggs should be refrigerated as soon as possible after purchase since the unprotected membrane may break while you are transporting them to your distribution place and thus be a good home for bacterial growth. Check carefully for leaky eggs and crack them into a bowl of water for storage for safest keeping, or use them immediately. Grade B eggs are slightly misshapen or have soft spots on the shell, and their yolks don't mound up as high as grade A egg yolks do when fried sunny-side up. Restaurants and bakeries use these cheaper eggs; you may as well take advantage of the savings, too.

COORDINATING

Members must take turns:
- Accepting and collating orders, money and returned egg cartons.
- Receiving or picking up orders. (If you pick up chickens, be sure to put them in leakproof containers—they drip, even frozen ones.)
- Distributing the orders to the members.

RAISING YOUR OWN

There is one more way to get chickens and eggs which is really the best way: grow your own. Before you go out and buy some chickens and build a hen house, check with your city hall to see if you are zoned for it and if you will need any licenses and permits. (This is the only time in this book you will be told to ask city hall for information. Usually they don't know what kind of permits you will need and will try to sell you everything. As a general rule, your suppliers will tell you if you need any permits in order to buy from them.)

Eggs and Chickens/How to Eat It

CHICKEN SOUP

Simmer together in a 5- to
6-quart pot until chicken is done:
1 chicken, cut up
10 cups water
2 to 3 onions, chopped
2 tablespoons salt
Bone chicken and break into
bite-sized pieces. Put the pieces
back into the soup.
Add to soup while still hot:
2 carrots, coarsely chopped
**2 to 3 stalks celery, coarsely
    chopped**
When carrots and celery are warm
through, serve immediately or
refrigerate. This soup tastes
better when it is a day or 2 old.
Serves 6 to 8

EGG DROP SOUP

Heat until simmering:
1 quart leftover chicken soup
Crack a little and slowly drizzle
into soup:
1 or 2 eggs
The egg must be added slowly
to the soup so that it will cook
instantly forming long strands.
Stir and serve.
Serves 4

TIJUANA SOUP

In a 4- to 5-quart pot, cover and
bring to a boil:
1 chicken, cut up
10 cups water
2 tablespoons salt
light sprinkle cayenne pepper
1 onion, quartered
Turn down heat and simmer for
30 minutes. Skim off fat. Add to
soup and cook 30 minutes more:
1 onion, chopped
1 to 2 stalks celery, chopped
2 medium-sized tomatoes, cut up
2 tablespoons sesame seeds
2 to 3 teaspoons ground cumin
1/4 to 1/2 cup brown rice
Serves 6 to 8

WALT'S CHICKEN
LIVER SOUP

Put in a saucepan and bring
to a boil:
1 quart water
1/2 pound chicken livers
**2 large crookneck squash, sliced
    in thick rounds**
4 medium-sized carrots, sliced
2 small onions
1 potato, diced
salt and pepper to taste

Cover, turn down heat and cook
for 20 minutes, or until livers
are cooked and carrots are soft.
Skim off fat before serving. This
recipe is enough for 2 people.
Give 1 onion to each.

RESTUFFED EGGS

Hard boil:
5 eggs
Slice eggs in half lengthwise and
remove yolks to a bowl.
Add to yolks and mix well:
**1 to 2 tablespoons mayonnaise
    or sour cream**
**1 tablespoon Worcestershire
    sauce or soy sauce**
Replace yolks in whites and
top with:
minced parsley, or
paprika, or
minced chives
Makes 10 snacks

MAYONNAISE

Beat together thoroughly:
2 raw egg yolks
1/2 teaspoon sea salt
1/4 teaspoon each cayenne
    pepper and paprika
1/8 teaspoon dry mustard
anything else you want
Add and beat again:
3 tablespoons vinegar or
    lemon juice
Add, drop by drop at first,
beating hard between additions:
2 cups vegetable oil

If your mayonnaise curdles, the
following procedure usually fixes
it. Have ready:
1 raw egg yolk
1 teaspoon oil
In a clean bowl, add oil to yolk
drop by drop, beating as you go.
Then add the curdled mayonnaise
in very small quantities until it is
mixed well. Your mayonnaise
should be thick and creamy.
Makes approximately 2 cups

CHEESE CUSTARD

Mix together:
2 cups milk
2 eggs, well beaten
1 cup (not packed) soft or hard
    grated cheese
salt to taste
paprika (optional)
Pour in buttered custard cups
and place in pan of hot water
1 inch deep. Bake at 350° 45 minutes, or until a knife inserted in
center comes out clean. Serve
on lettuce.
Serves 2 to 4

SCRAMBLED EGGS PLUS

Beat together well:
6 eggs
1/2 cup water
Add to eggs one of the following:
1/2 cup wheat germ
1/3 cup powdered milk
1 cup grated cheese
1/2 cup sunflower seeds
1 cup cashew nuts
1/2 cup toasted sesame seeds
1 orange or grapefruit, peeled
    and chopped
Pour into preheated pan:
1 tablespoon oil
Pour eggs into oiled, heated pan
and cook until done.
Serves 3 to 4

EGG FOO YONG

Sauté in a cast-iron frying pan:
2 tablespoons oil
1 cup boned, cooked chicken
    (optional)
1/4 cup mung bean sprouts
1 small onion, chopped
1 stalk celery, minced
2 parsley sprigs, chopped
Drain off liquid and reserve.
Combine vegetables in a bowl
with:
6 eggs, slightly beaten
Preheat in a frying pan:
2 to 3 tablespoons oil
Pour the egg mixture into the
pan. Brown one side and flip to
brown the other side.
Combine and heat:
reserved liquid from vegetables
3 tablespoons soy sauce
2 teaspoons cornstarch or
    tapioca flour
Pour over the egg foo yong. The
cornstarch acts as a thickener; it
has no flavor after it is cooked.
Serves 4

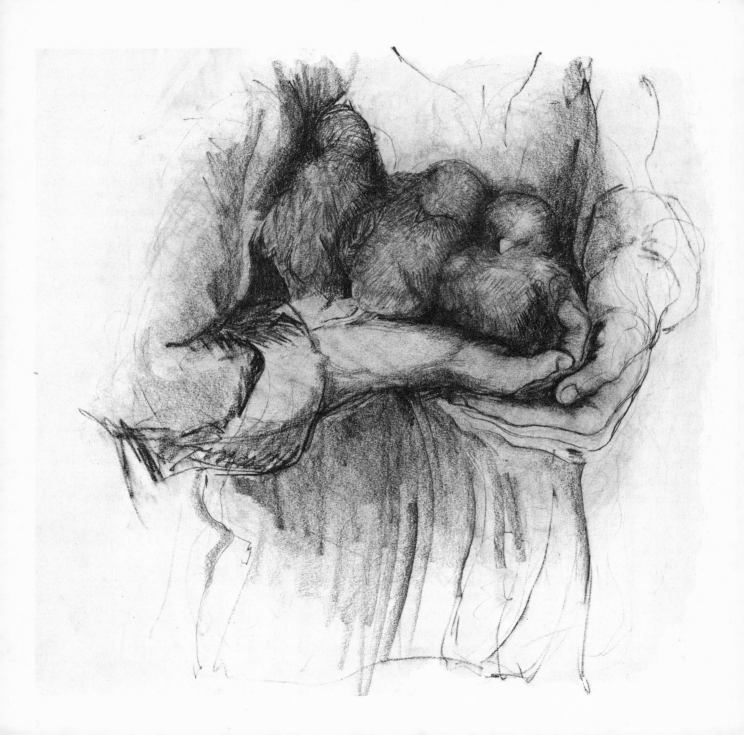

PICKLE OMELETTE

Sauté until tender in:
vegetable oil
1 to 2 potatoes, finely diced
Pour over potatoes:
3 or 4 eggs, beaten with
2 tablespoons milk or water
Cook over low heat, stirring
occasionally. At the last minute,
stir in:
1/2 cup grated cheese
salt and pepper to taste
1 pickle, chopped
onion, mushrooms and/or
    bell pepper, chopped
    (optional)
Serves 2

HIGH-PROTEIN OMELETTE

Mix together:
1 cup cottage cheese
4 eggs
dash each salt, cinnamon and
    nutmeg
1 tablespoon honey
Pour into hot buttered pan
and scramble.
Serves 2

QUICK DINNER EGGS

Sauté until onion is soft:
1 onion, chopped
1 tablespoon oil
Add to pan and scramble:
5 eggs, beaten
Sprinkle on top:
salt, powdered ginger and pepper
Serve on:
brown rice with a sprinkle
    of soy sauce
if desired.
Serves 2 to 3

SOYBEAN EGG SOUFFLÉ

Run through meat grinder:
1 cup cooked soybeans
Sauté:
1 yellow onion, chopped
Whip until stiff but not dry:
3 egg whites
Beat until smooth:
3 egg yolks
Add to beaten yolks:
salt and cayenne pepper to taste
Chop and cook:
vegetables of choice (optional)
Fold all ingredients together and
place in a buttered baking dish.
Bake at 350° for 30 minutes.
Serves 4

SWEET AND SOUR EGGS

Sauté in oil:
1 large onion, chopped
5 garlic cloves, minced
Add to pan and scramble:
5 eggs, beaten
sprinkle of salt and
    powdered ginger
Serve over:
brown rice (about 1/2 cup per
    person)
Top with the following sauce.
Heat in a saucepan:
1/2 cup stock or water
1-1/2 tablespoons molasses
1-1/2 tablespoons apple cider
    vinegar
Add to sauce and simmer until
it thickens:
1 to 1-1/2 tablespoons whole-
    wheat flour
Serves 2

Eggs and Chickens/How to Eat It

CHICKEN AYALA

Oil the outsides and salt the
cavities of:
2 whole chickens
Mix together and stuff the
cavities with:
1-1/2 cups cooked brown rice
**1/2 pound mushrooms, sliced
and sautéed**
**salt, pepper, savory, sage, thyme
and parsley to taste**
Sprinkle on chickens:
**salt, pepper, savory, sage, thyme
and minced garlic**
Sew up chickens and place in
a roasting pan. Pour into pan:
2 cups stock or water
Place in 350° oven. When pan
liquid boils, cover and cook for
2 hours, uncovering the pan the
last 15 minutes. Baste occasionally
during cooking. Add vegetables to
the pan, if desired. When the
chickens are cooked, add to the
pan juices to make gravy:
2 tablespoons whole-wheat flour
Serves 8

MS. ROSEMARY PAPRIKA'S CHICKEN

Roll:
1 chicken, cut up, in
**1-1/2 cups whole-wheat flour
mixed with salt and cayenne
pepper**
Place the pieces in a hot oiled
frying pan. Shake heavily
over the chicken:
rosemary and paprika
Brown the chicken on 1 side,
turn it and shake rosemary and
paprika on the other side. Cover
and cook over low heat about
20 minutes. If chicken is not
cooked in this time, turn again
and cook until done.
Serves 4

BAKED CHICKEN WITH WHEAT GERM

Have ready:
1 chicken, cut up
6 tablespoons butter, melted
1-1/2 cups wheat germ
Roll each piece of chicken in the
melted butter and then in the
wheat germ, coating well. Arrange
chicken pieces on a cookie sheet
and bake at 350° for 1 hour. Salt
and serve.
Serves 4

TUNISIAN CHICKEN

Have ready:
1 whole chicken
Smear outside and cavity of
chicken with:
salt, pepper and olive oil
Tie chicken for roasting. Heat in
a heavy pot:
1/4 cup oil
Brown chicken as much as
possible, adding to the pot
when halfway finished:
1 onion, chopped
When finished browning add
to the pot:
1 cup or less water
2 to 3 tomatoes, chopped
Cook a while, covered.
Grill over flame until skin is
black, then slice:
1 to 2 green peppers
Peel off the skins and put slices
into the pot with the chicken.
Add:
1 chili pepper, seeded and sliced
Cook 40 minutes, basting often.
When the chicken is done, cut
into serving pieces and serve over
rice, pouring the sauce over it.
The grilled green peppers give it
an intoxicating Mediterranean
fragrance.
Serves 4

SAN ANTONIO ROAD CHICKEN

Have ready:
1 chicken, cut up
salt and powdered ginger
flour
oil
Sprinkle chicken pieces with salt and ginger and roll in flour. Brown in oil in a 4-quart pot. Add to the pot:
1 or more onions, cut in rings
5 garlic cloves, minced
approximately 1 cup dried pitted prunes
1 cup raisins
1/2 to 3/4 cup dried apricots
2 to 3 tablespoons sesame seeds
1 cup brown rice
1 to 2 slices lemon
cinnamon to taste
water to within 1-1/2 inches of top of chicken
Bring water to a boil. Turn heat down and simmer 40 minutes to 1 hour, or until chicken is done. Remove chicken from pot and spoon some rice, fruit and sauce onto each plate. Place chicken pieces on top and serve.
Serves 4

HOT (OPTIONAL) CHICKEN STEW

Have ready:
1 chicken, cut up
salt
cayenne pepper
whole-wheat flour
Sprinkle chicken with salt. Then sprinkle sparingly with cayenne and roll in flour. Brown chicken in:
oil
chopped garlic to taste
Sprinkle generously with:
cumin powder
Place chicken and garlic in a heavy pot with:
2 carrots, sliced
1 onion, chopped
1 potato, sliced
salt and cayenne pepper to taste
2 to 3 tomatoes, chopped
1 hot red chili pepper, chopped (optional)
1-1/2 cups chicken or beef broth
Bring to a boil, cover and simmer over low heat for 40 minutes to 1 hour, or until chicken is done. Whole-wheat flour may be added to pan liquid to make gravy.
Serves 4

PEANUT BUTTER CHICKEN

Blend together well to make a marinade:
1/2 cup soy sauce
1/2 cup crunchy peanut butter
1/4 cup chablis
1/4 cup soybean oil or safflower oil
2 tablespoons blackstrap molasses
1 to 2 tablespoons curry powder
1 to 2 garlic cloves, chopped
1/2 teaspoon salt
juice of 2 lemons
Soak in marinade:
2 chickens, cut up
Combine chicken and marinade with:
2 to 3 cups cooked rice
currants (optional)
Bake for 1-1/2 hours at 350°.
Variations:
Refrigerate chicken in the marinade overnight and grill, basting frequently with the marinade.
Place chicken and marinade in a Dutch oven on top of the stove and cook until done, stirring often.
Serves 8

INDIAN CHICKEN WITH PEACHES

Simmer 5 minutes, then remove from heat:
1/2 cup butter or oil
2 teaspoons or more curry powder
Stir into above mixture:
2 medium-sized onions, finely chopped
4 tablespoons wine vinegar
1/2 cup water, including some soy sauce to taste
2 to 3 tablespoons honey
Place in baking pan:
1 chicken, cut up
3 to 4 peaches, halved
the butter mixture
Bake at 400° for 1 hour, or until done, basting and turning every 15 minutes. Serve over rice. This is good to serve to a new friend.
Serves 4

ORANGE JUICE CHICKEN

Have ready:
1 chicken, cut up
flour
oil
Shake chicken pieces in flour and fry in oil until skin is crusty.
Sauté with chicken:
2 garlic cloves, chopped
Cut into eighths:
1 large yellow onion
Stick in each onion section:
1 whole clove
Place above ingredients in a 4-quart pot. Pour in:
1-1/2 cups orange juice
1/2 cup stock
Then add:
1 bay leaf
1/4 teaspoon thyme
1 teaspoon salt
3 tablespoons nutritional yeast or whole-wheat flour
1 tablespoon soy flour (optional)
1 large carrot, chopped
1/4 cup toasted sesame seeds (optional)
1/2 pound mushrooms, sliced (optional)
Bake at 350° for 1 hour, or until chicken is tender.
Serves 4

CURRY FROM LEFTOVER CHICKEN

Mix together in a 3-quart pot:
1 cup or more chicken meat from leftover baked or fried chicken, cut in bite-sized pieces
3 cups cooked brown rice
1/4 cup diced green onion, or
1 small onion, chopped and sautéed
1 to 2 garlic cloves, chopped
2 teaspoons curry powder
1/4 pound mushrooms, chopped and sautéed
1 tablespoon lime juice
1/2 cup currants
1/4 to 1/2 cup chopped or slivered almonds
1/4 to 1/2 cup shredded coconut
Bake at 350° 40 minutes, or until warmed through.
Serves 4

BERKELEY CHICKEN WITH TARRAGON GRAVY

Brown in a large casserole or
cast-iron pot:
1 chicken, cut up
Mix in with chicken:
2 large onions, sliced in rings
Mix together and pour over
chicken:
2 cups stock or water
3 tablespoons whole-wheat flour
1/2 tablespoon salt
3 tablespoons nutritional yeast
2-1/2 teaspoons or more tarragon
3 tablespoons finely chopped
   parsley
Cover and bake at 350° for
1 hour. Serve with plain yogurt
and brown rice. You can mix the
yogurt with the gravy. If there
is any leftover gravy, serve it
over vegetables on rice or over
potatoes or homemade bread.
Serves 4

FOWL PINEAPPLE

Make a marinade with:
3 cups pineapple chunks
1 cup pineapple juice
2 tablespoons freshly grated
   ginger, or
1 teaspoon powdered ginger
1 cup soy sauce
4 garlic cloves, minced
1 onion, chopped
Place in the marinade for at least
2 hours:
2 chickens, cut up
Remove chicken from marinade
and brown in oil in an ovenproof
pan. Pour the marinade over the
browned chicken pieces and
bring to a simmer. Then put the
pan in a 325° oven and bake
for 1 hour.

OVERNIGHT CHICKEN

Place in a 3-quart Dutch oven:
1 whole chicken
Pour or place around it:
1 28-ounce can peaches or
   tomatoes
1 cup rice
2 large onions, cut in rings
cinnamon, salt and other
   spices of choice
1 cup water
Bake at 200° overnight. Eat
for brunch.

HILLEGASS SPICED RICE AND RAISINS

Put into a pot:
1-1/4 cups brown rice
1/4 to 1/2 cup broken noodles
dash salt
1-1/4 teaspoons cinnamon
1/4 cup garbanzo beans,
   soaked overnight
1/4 teaspoon cardamom
1/2 cup or more raisins
1 large onion, chopped
1 teaspoon allspice
1/4 teaspoon ginger
Pour over contents of pot:
2-1/2 cups bouillon, stock or
   water
Bring to a boil, cover and turn
heat as low as possible. Cook
about 55 minutes, or until the
liquid is absorbed. While rice is
cooking, fry until done:
4 pieces (breasts or legs) chicken,
   deboned, seasoned with salt
   and powdered ginger
Place chicken into the pot with
the cooked rice and serve.
Serves 2 to 3

CHICKEN INDIA

Cut in bite-sized pieces:
4 chicken breasts, boned
Sprinkle on chicken:
salt, ginger and curry powder
In frying pan, sauté in:
oil
1 large onion, chopped
6 to 8 garlic cloves, chopped
Add chicken to pan and continue
frying until done.
Add to pan:
1-1/2 cups stock, milk or water
1 teaspoon or more curry powder
salt to taste
1 tablespoon whole-wheat flour
1 green pepper, chopped
1 carrot, sliced
Cover and simmer until carrots
are tender, about 20 minutes.
Serve over rice or buckwheat
groats and sliced cucumbers
dressed with a mixture of:
1/2 cup yogurt
1/3 cup honey
Serves 4

CHICKEN BREASTS
A LA SUISSE

Have ready:
3 whole chicken breasts, boned
    and halved
6 thin slices smoked meat
6 thin slices Swiss cheese
Place meat and cheese slices on
chicken breasts and roll like a
jelly roll. Fasten with a toothpick.
Sauté breasts in:
4 tablespoons butter
Lower heat and add to pan:
1 cup dry white wine
salt and pepper to taste
Cover and cook slowly until
chicken is tender, about 20 minutes. Remove chicken to platter
and keep warm.
Put in pan and cook 2 minutes:
1 tablespoon chopped onion
Mix together and add to pan:
1/2 pint sour cream
2 egg yolks
Heat, but do not boil. Serve
separately as a sauce.
Serves 3 to 4

GAR DOO GAI
(Chinese Chicken Salad)

Sauté in:
2 tablespoons peanut oil
3 chicken breasts, boned and
    cut in bite-sized pieces
Remove from pan and reserve.
In same pan, heat until very hot:
1 tablespoon peanut oil
Add and stir until the
grains get hard,
about 2 minutes:
1/2 cup cooked rice
Add to rice and heat thoroughly:
1/4 cup chicken broth
1 tablespoon soy sauce
Then add:
2 cups shredded lettuce
1/2 cup sliced green onion
2 tablespoons chutney
2 tablespoons toasted sesame
    seeds
the sautéed chicken
Toss just enough to blend well
and serve.
Serves 3 to 4

Eggs and Chickens/How to Eat It

RIZZOTO

Sauté in:
oil
2 large onions, chopped
1 cup raw rice
until onions are translucent and rice is browned. Place browned rice and onions in a saucepan with:
1 garlic clove, minced
2 cups chicken broth
pinch saffron
Bring to boil, cover and simmer until rice is cooked (about 20 minutes). Meanwhile fry and cut into bite-sized pieces:
3/4 pound chicken livers
In a greased casserole place layers of the rice mixture, chicken livers and:
1/2 pound grated Parmesan cheese
Bake at 350°, uncovered, for 30 minutes.
Serves 2 to 3

PIROSHKI

To Make Filling:
Sauté separately:
1 pound chicken hearts, or
1 pound ground beef
1 yellow onion, chopped
If using chicken hearts, put through a meat grinder after they are cooked. Mix meat and onions in a bowl with:
1/4 cup sesame seeds
1/2 cup chopped walnuts or pecans
salt to taste
To Make Dough:
Mix together with hands or machine, adding ice water until dough can be easily handled:
4 cups whole-wheat flour
1 teaspoon salt
1-1/2 cups butter, softened
2 eggs, beaten (optional)
approximately 1/2 cup ice water
Roll out 1/8 inch thick and cut in 3- to 4-inch squares or circles. Place a heaping tablespoon or more filling on half the rounds. Cover with remaining rounds and seal with fingers or fork tines. Bake on a cookie sheet at 350° about 45 minutes, or until dough is done.
Serves 4 to 6
A yeasted bread dough will do just as well.

BARBECUED CHICKEN WINGS

Mix together:
1/2 cup soy sauce
1 to 2 tablespoons toasted sesame oil
juice of 1 lemon
2 tablespoons honey (optional)
1 to 2 garlic cloves, crushed
salt to taste
Pour marinade over:
2 pounds chicken wings or other poultry, meat or fish, or vegetables
Marinate at least 10 minutes. Barbecue over hot coals until done.
Serves 4

CHICKEN GIZZARD STEW

Place in heavy pot:
1 pound chicken gizzards
2 to 3 tomatoes
1 onion, chopped
seasoned salt to taste
Simmer, stirring often, until gizzards are done. Serves 2 to 4, depending on what else you have with it.

JEAN KEITH'S DIRTY RICE

Sauté:
1 pound chicken giblets
Put giblets through meat grinder
and place in pot with:
1 yellow onion, chopped, or
2 green onions, chopped
Add to pot:
1 bouillon cube dissolved in
1 cup water
1-1/2 cups rice
1 teaspoon curry powder
salt and cayenne pepper
   to taste
Finally add:
2 cups water
Cover with tight-fitting lid and
cook 40 minutes, or until water
is absorbed by the rice.
Serves 4 to 6

MARGUERITES

Fold together, combining
thoroughly:
4 egg whites, beaten stiff
1-1/2 cups white sugar
1 teaspoon vanilla extract
2 cups chocolate bits
1 cup chopped nuts
Spoon mixture onto buttered
cookie sheets in spoonful-sized
drops. Place in a preheated 350°
oven. Turn oven off and let
stand overnight.

ORANGE JUICE CHIFFON

Place in an ovenproof 2-quart pot:
3 tablespoons whole-wheat flour
3 egg yolks, beaten
juice of 1 lemon
1 cup freshly squeezed orange
   juice
1/4 cup or less mild honey
Cook and stir over low heat until
mixture thickens.
Whip until stiff but not dry:
3 egg whites
Fold egg whites into egg-yolk
mixture. Place in a 400° oven 10
minutes. When it is done it looks
like lemon chiffon. This recipe
may also be made with puréed
strawberries or used as a pie
filling.
Serves 4

FORGOTTEN TORTE

Fold together:
5 egg whites, beaten stiff
1/4 teaspoon salt
1/2 teaspoon cream of tartar
1-1/2 cups white sugar
1 teaspoon vanilla extract
Spoon onto a buttered pan and
place in a preheated 450° oven.
Turn oven off and let stand in the
oven overnight. Serve alone, or
with ice cream or fruit.

SNORFY CUSTARD

Beat together in a 2-quart bowl:
3 eggs, slightly beaten
2-3/4 cups milk
1/4 cup instant powdered milk
1/3 cup brown sugar
1-1/2 teaspoons vanilla extract
generous pinch salt
Pour into 6 custard cups. Place
the cups in a baking dish and
pour hot water into the dish to
a depth of 1 inch. Place in a 350°
oven for 45 minutes to 1 hour, or
until a knife inserted at the edge
of a cup comes out clean. Good
served warm or chilled.
Serves 6

CHOCOLATE MOUSSE

Whip until stiff:
4 egg whites
Beat until smooth:
4 egg yolks
Melt together over low flame:
1/4 cup chocolate bits
1 tablespoon water
Mix melted chocolate into egg
yolks and then fold in beaten
whites. Freeze for about 3 hours.
This tastes like rich ice cream.
Serves 4
Note: This recipe cannot
be successfully doubled.

Beef and Lamb

Our basic experiences with these animals have been short-lived. It is often difficult to find a supplier who can sell you meat at a savings. We have had meat from the California Agrarian League (self-described as a hip co-op). And we almost got meat from some people who were found to be cattle rustlers. However, if you do want to get meat for your conspiracy, you will need:

• A freezer (and money for its electricity bill) or rental freezer locker to store what members won't eat at once.

• Someone who knows about beef or lamb, so he can recognize a good animal on the hoof or in sides or quarters, or a supplier you can trust. (USDA grading costs 3 cents per pound extra and only measures the fat content.)

• Members with enough money to buy meat for a month ahead.

• Members who will eat all the different cuts of meat and the innards.

FINDING A SUPPLIER

To find a supplier you should: look in the yellow pages for dealers in halves and quarters; write or call your county livestock association; ask an employee of a local health food store that carries beef and lamb where the meat comes from, and send some of your members out to the farm to ask the same kinds of questions that you asked at the chicken farm; and if all else fails, ask a local grocery or health food store for a discount on quantity purchases.

COORDINATING BEEF AND LAMB

Members will have to decide how much to charge for each cut since you will be buying the entire quantity at one price per pound, too high for chuck and extremely low for T-bone. You will need to compensate or no one will take the normally cheaper cuts. Remember, if you buy a whole cow, only about half of it is edible. The coordinator should: take orders and money, and buy the meat; arrange to transport the animal or section thereof; make sure someone will cut, wrap and label the pieces and put them into a freezer; and make sure each member gets what he paid for.

Beef and Lamb/How to Eat It

SWEET LAMB CHOPS

Have ready:
2 shoulder lamb chops
salt and pepper
1/2 cup honey or less
Sprinkle lamb chops with salt and pepper and coat with honey. Coat the bottom of a frying pan with:
1/2 cup apple juice
Place the chops in the frying pan with the apple juice and cook on both sides, adding more apple juice as needed. Sprinkle with more salt and pepper to taste. Serve with apple slices and potatoes that have been steamed together.
Serves 2

CURRIED LAMB CHOPS WITHOUT A SAUCE

Sprinkle:
2 shoulder lamb chops with salt, pepper and curry powder
Fry, broil or bake until chops are done.
Serves 2

FAST DISAPPEARING LEG OF LAMB

Have ready:
1 4- to 6-pound leg of lamb, preferably boneless
3 garlic cloves, sliced
Make 1/2-inch deep slits in the lamb in 3-inch intervals. Push a garlic slice into each slit. Place the lamb fat side up in a baking dish. Arrange over the lamb:
1 to 2 onions, cut in rings (optional)
Bake in a 200° or cooler oven, uncovered, for 5 to 8 hours, or until done. Baste occasionally, if necessary. You can cook this overnight without overdoing it.
Serves 5 to 8

LAMB CURRY

Sauté, turning with a wooden spoon until golden:
2-1/2 pounds boned lamb, cut in 2-inch cubes, in
1/2 cup butter
Remove lamb from pan. In same pan, sauté until onions are translucent:
1-1/2 large onions, finely chopped
1 garlic clove, mashed
3 celery stalks, finely chopped
Combine with sautéed vegetables:
1-1/2 cups coconut milk, or
2/3 cup milk, 1/2 cup flaked coconut and 2 tablespoons butter simmered together and pressed through a fine sieve
1-1/2 cups chicken stock
Blend together the following spices (this is called Kari blend) and add to vegetable mixture:
3 tablespoons curry powder
1/4 teaspoon each powdered ginger, turmeric and paprika
1/2 teaspoon cayenne pepper
salt and pepper to taste
Add to vegetables:
6 tablespoons seed-free raisins
Add lamb cubes to vegetables and cook over low heat until meat is tender, stirring occasionally. Remove from heat. Stir into meat and vegetables:
6 tablespoons yogurt
Correct seasoning and serve with boiled rice and:
chopped nuts
coconut
chutney
anything else yummy
Serves 4

COUSCOUS

Brown in olive oil:

1 pound breast or shoulder of lamb, cut up

Drain off fat.

Peel and cut in quarters:

a few carrots

a few onions

a few turnips

Add vegetables to pot with lamb.

Stir in with wooden spoon:

3/4 cup tomato paste (6-ounce can)

Stir and cook 20 minutes. Add to pot and cook covered 1 hour:

1 fresh or dried hot chili pepper, minced

oregano, coriander, garlic, bay leaf, salt to taste

4 cups water

Add to pot and cook until done:

2 to 3 zucchini or other vegetable, sliced in 1-inch pieces

Add to pot or serve separately:

1 cup cooked garbanzo beans (optional)

Serve copiously over couscous, rice or cracked wheat.

Serves 4 to 6

LONG-COOKING JAPANESE EGGPLANT STUFFED WITH LAMB

Cut off the tops and scoop out the seeds of:

6 to 8 Japanese eggplants

Use scooped-out portions, fried with other vegetables, as a side dish. Mix together:

1/2 cup raw rice

1 pound ground lamb

2 garlic cloves, minced

1 onion, chopped

salt and cayenne pepper to taste

Spoon mixture into hollowed-out eggplants. Place stuffed eggplants in a baking dish. Mix together:

2 cups tomato juice or sauce, or 3 tomatoes, puréed

1/4 cup wine vinegar

1 tablespoon chicken bouillon

2 tablespoons brown sugar or honey

Pour tomato mixture over eggplant, adding water to cover if necessary. Bake at least 5 hours in a 250° to 300° oven, or until about two-thirds of the sauce is absorbed and the rice is tender. This recipe works well with squash or bell peppers, too.

Serves 3 or 4

BABOOTIE

Brown:

1 pound ground lamb

Drain off excess fat.

Add to lamb and sauté:

1 onion, chopped

Put in pan with the lamb and simmer for 20 to 30 minutes:

1 to 2 garlic cloves, finely chopped

1 cup tomato sauce

1 tablespoon brown sugar

1 tablespoon curry powder

1 tablespoon vinegar

salt to taste

cayenne pepper to taste

Add to pan, stir in and simmer another 10 minutes until bananas are warm but not mushy:

1 or 2 firm bananas, sliced

3 or 4 apples, cored and chopped

8 to 16 apricot halves, canned or fresh

1/4 to 1/2 cup slivered almonds (optional)

Serve over rice.

Serves 4 to 6

BEEF OR LAMB KEDGEREE

In a large pot, sauté until done:
1 pound ground beef or lamb
1 onion, chopped
1 to 2 garlic cloves, chopped
Drain off fat. Place in pot with
meat:
1/2 cup raisins
1 cup soaked and drained
**   lentils or partially cooked ones**
6 cups beef broth
1 teaspoon cinnamon
1 teaspoon ground cloves, or
6 whole cloves
seeds from 1 cardamom pod
**   (optional)**
Cover and cook for about 1-1/2
hours, depending on whether
lentils are partially cooked. Add
to pot:
1 cup raw brown rice
Cover and simmer for 40 minutes,
or until rice is done. If there is
liquid remaining after the rice is
cooked, remove the cover and let
it steam off. Or add bread
crumbs to soak it up.
Serves 4

RED COOKED
MAIN COURSE

Quickly fry over high heat for
1 minute in oil:
1/4 to 1/2 pound meat of choice,
**   cut in strips**
Add to pan and continue cooking over high heat until onion is
soft and browned:
1 onion, chopped, or
1 bunch green onions, chopped
1 teaspoon ground ginger, or
3 to 4 slices fresh ginger root
Lower heat and add:
1/2 cup soy sauce
1 tablespoon sherry
1 tablespoon brown sugar
approximately 2 cups water
Simmer 40 to 45 minutes. Add
to pan choice of the following
and simmer 15 to 20 minutes
more:
1/4 pound snow peas
water chestnuts, sliced
bamboo shoots, sliced diagonally
Chinese mushrooms or fresh
**   mushrooms, sliced**
mung bean sprouts
fresh peas or beans
celery, sliced diagonally
lotus root, sliced diagonally

Mix together and add to pan,
stirring constantly:
2 tablespoons cornstarch
1/4 cup water
Cook until gravy thickens and is
translucent again.
Serves 2 to 4

OVERNIGHT ROAST

Put in a 3- to 5-quart pot (if
meat is fatty, place fat side up to
prevent juices from evaporating):
1 3-pound chuck roast, browned
2 pounds tomatoes, peeled
**   and quartered**
2 large onions, cut in rings
1 teaspoon cinnamon
2 garlic cloves, peeled and cut up
2 cardamom pods
salt and cayenne pepper to taste
leftover vegetables, cut up
leftover grains
Place pot, uncovered, in a 200°
oven around sundown. Enjoy this
dish for brunch the next day.
Serves 6

LEFTOVERS CREOLE

Sauté:
1 onion, chopped
1 garlic clove, minced
2 tablespoons oil
Place in a 4- to 5-quart pot
and add:
2 to 3 soft tomatoes
3 tablespoons tomato paste
1/4 cup water
1 teaspoon salt
1/4 teaspoon thyme
1 bay leaf, crumbled
dash cayenne pepper
1 celery stalk, chopped
1 carrot, chopped
1 to 2 cups leftover beef,
    chicken or fish, or
2 6-1/2-ounce cans tuna
mushrooms and canned corn are
    nice, too, if you have some
Simmer for 25 minutes and serve.
Serves 4

SQUASH STEW

In a large pot combine:
2 pounds beef stew meat, cubed
1 large tomato, cut up
1/2 teaspoon sweet basil
Cover and cook over low heat
for 1 hour.

To the pot add:
1 zucchini, cut in large pieces
1 yellow crookneck squash, cut
    in large pieces
1/2 green cabbage, cut in small
    pieces
water, if necessary
Cover and cook 45 minutes.
Lower heat and add:
4 tablespoons sour cream
salt to taste
Vegetables come out as if puréed,
making a delicious gravy.
Serves 4

VITAMIN A STEW

Place in a 4-quart pot:
2 pounds beef stew meat, cubed
2 medium-sized yams, peeled and
    cut in 1/2-inch slices
2 yellow crookneck squash,
    chopped in large chunks
1 medium-sized onion, chopped
1/2 teaspoon sweet basil
1 cup water
Cover and cook over medium
heat for 1-1/2 hours, stirring
occasionally to avoid sticking.
Lower heat and simmer for
10 minutes. Just before serving,
mix in:
4 tablespoons sour cream
salt to taste
Serves 4 to 6

BEEF WITH DRIED FRUIT AND RICE

Brown on all sides in large oiled
skillet:
1 2-pound chuck roast
Add to the pan:
3/4 cup water
Cover and place in a 350° oven
2-1/2 hours. At the same time
the meat goes in the oven start
soaking:
1/4 pound dried apricots or
    prunes, in
water to cover
When the meat has finished cooking, add drained soaked fruit and:
1 cup raw rice
2 cups boiling water
juice and cut-up rind of 1 lemon
cinnamon and nutmeg to taste
Return to oven and cook 45 minutes, or until rice is done.
Then add:
salt to taste
Serves 4 to 5

MEAT-STUFFED PUMPKIN

With a sharp knife, cut a circular top of about 5 inches in diameter out of:
1 small pumpkin
Save the top for a lid. Scoop out the seeds and scrape inside of pumpkin clean. Place pumpkin in a large pot and add:
boiling salted water to cover
Bring water to boil again and simmer until pumpkin meat is almost tender when pierced with a fork, about 30 minutes. Pumpkin should be firm enough to still hold its shape well. Carefully remove pumpkin from water, drain and pat dry. Sprinkle inside of pumpkin lightly with:
salt
Heat in a large frying pan:
2 tablespoons salad oil
Add to pan and fry until meat is brown and crumbly:
2 pounds ground chuck
2-1/2 cups chopped onions
Remove from pan.

Mix together, then mix well with meat and onions and cook over low heat for 15 minutes, stirring frequently:
2-1/2 teaspoons salt
2 teaspoons olive oil
2 teaspoons oregano
1 teaspoon vinegar
1 teaspoon freshly ground pepper
dash cayenne pepper
2 garlic cloves, minced
3/4 cup currants
1/3 cup pimiento-stuffed green olives, chopped
1 cup tomato sauce
Remove from heat and allow to cool slightly.
Mix into meat mixture as thoroughly as possible:
3 eggs, beaten
Fill pumpkin with meat stuffing, packing it firmly, and cover loosely with pumpkin lid. Place in a shallow greased pan and bake at 350° for 1 hour.
Serves 4 to 6

LASAGNE

Fry:
1 to 2 pounds ground beef, in
2 tablespoons olive oil
Drain off fat. Fry in pan with meat, adding oil as needed:
1 onion, chopped
2 garlic cloves, chopped

Add to pan and simmer 1-1/2 hours:
1 28-ounce can tomato purée
1 6-ounce can tomato paste
3/4 cup water (optional)
1/2 teaspoon salt
1/2 teaspoon cayenne pepper
1-1/2 to 3 teaspoons oregano
1 cup sliced mushrooms or eggplant (optional)
Have ready:
1 pound ricotta cheese
1-1/2 pounds mozzarella cheese, sliced
12 to 15 cooked lasagne noodles
Place 3 lasagne noodles on the bottom of a greased 2- to 3-quart casserole dish and pour some of the meat sauce over them. Top with dabs of ricotta cheese and then with mozzarella cheese slices to cover the casserole. Repeat the layering process until all the ingredients are used up. You may want to put 3 noodles on top.
Sprinkle top with:
1/4 cup grated Parmesan cheese
Bake at 350° for 45 minutes to 1 hour, or until cheese is goopy.
Serves 8

Beef and Lamb/How to Eat It

FLIEG'S GOOP
A LA HOLLANDER

Brown together:
1 pound ground meat of choice
1 large or 2 small onions, chopped
2 to 3 celery stalks, chopped
Drain off fat. Place in a large pot
and simmer 30 minutes:
the browned beef, onions and
    celery
1 28-ounce can tomato purée
seasonings to taste, including
    salt, pepper, cayenne pepper
    (just a little), garlic, sweet
    basil, sage, thyme, oregano,
    cumin (a little), rosemary and
    other spices as the fancy
    strikes you
2 cups corn kernels
2 cups green beans, chopped
1 green pepper, sliced
mushrooms, if you have them
Serve over rice or pasta. Serves
4 of me or 12 normal people as
part of a regular meal with salad,
etc. Ingredients can be left out or
new ones added to taste. The
spirit of experimentation is not
dead!

YUMMIER-THAN-EXPECTED
MEATLOAF

Mix together and shape into loaf:
1-1/2 pounds ground beef
1 cup wheat germ
1/2 cup tomato sauce
1 onion, chopped
1 egg
1-1/2 teaspoons salt
1/4 teaspoon cayenne pepper
Place loaf in an 8 x 8-inch pan.
Mix together and pour over loaf:
1/2 cup tomato sauce
3/4 cup water
2 tablespoons brown sugar
1 tablespoon vinegar
Bake at 350° for 1-1/4 hours.
Serves 4 to 6
Note:This works using meat-soy
blend, too.

CABBAGE ROLLS

Have ready:
1 medium-sized head cabbage
boiling water
Pour boiling water over cabbage
to cover. Let stand 5 minutes,
drain and core. Leaves will now
separate easily. Drain leaves on
absorbent paper.

Combine and shape into meatballs:
1-1/2 pounds ground beef
1 egg
1/4 cup bread crumbs
salt and pepper to taste
Place 1 meatball in the center of
each cabbage leaf and roll up.
Place rolled packets close together
in a baking dish. Mix together
until smooth and pour over
cabbage rolls:
1/2 cup light corn or other sweet
    syrup like ribbon cane, or
1/4 cup honey or corn syrup
    diluted with 1/4 cup apricot
    preserves
1 cup tomato catsup or tomato
    sauce
1 teaspoon fresh lemon juice
Bake at 350° for 1-1/2 hours. If
you leave the cabbage rolls uncovered they will look glazed
when done, but you will have to
check them several times to make
sure there is enough liquid in the
pan (add water if necessary). If
the baking dish is covered, they
won't look as nice, but they
won't need attention either.
Serves 4 to 6

TAMALE PIE

To Make Filling:
Sauté:
1 pound ground beef or ground
     sautéed chicken hearts
1/2 to 1 cup chopped onion
Drain off fat. Add to pan with
meat and onion and simmer 30
minutes:
2 cups canned tomatoes, or
3 large fresh tomatoes, quartered
1/2 teaspoon salt
1 garlic clove, chopped
1 to 2 tablespoons chili powder
Add to pan and warm through:
grated cheese (optional)
corn kernels (optional)
pitted black olives (optional)

To Make Crust:
Put in a 2-quart pot and stir for
about 15 minutes over medium
heat:
2-1/2 cups water
1 teaspoon salt
1 teaspoon chili powder
3/4 cup cornmeal
1/2 cup millet meal

Crust is done when it gets very
thick and starts to boil. Spread
crust on the bottom and halfway
up the sides of a 10x6-inch flat-
bottomed pan. Pour on the filling,
smoothing where necessary. Put
any leftover crust and/or some
cheese on top, if desired. Bake at
350° for 45 minutes.
Serves 4 to 6

TONGUE IN WINE SAUCE

Boil, 30 minutes less than
required cooking time (normally
1 hour per pound):
1 pickled beef tongue, not more
     than 3 pounds
(If your regular meat source does
not carry pickled tongues, try a
Kosher butcher.) Drain water off,
skin and slice. Combine for
sauce:
1-1/2 cups red wine
2 to 3 teaspoons dry mustard
1/4 to 1/3 cup currant jelly
1/4 cup raisins
1/4 cup walnuts
Place tongue slices in sauce and
simmer until tender.
Serves 6 to 8

GEREUSCH
(Swabian Stewed Lungs
and Heart)

Put into a deep pot:
2 pounds lungs and
1 heart of veal or lamb
1 onion, sliced
2 cooking tomatoes, cut up
1 beef bouillon cube
salt to taste
water to cover
Bring to a boil and stew for 1 to
1-1/4 hours. (The lung is
impossible to cut when raw;
don't try!) This cooking time
hardens and sterilizes the lung,
which is very important. Remove
lung and heart from the broth
and cut in 1/2-inch dice, discard-
ing bronchi, trachea, etc. Return
the diced meat to the broth and
stew for an additional 45
minutes.
Blend together and slowly mix in
to thicken the stew:
3 tablespoons whole-wheat flour
1/4 cup broth from stew
Serve over broad egg noodles or
spaetzle (page 88).
Serves 4

Fish

Getting fish requires special care. Most fish is frozen immediately after it is caught and it should not be allowed to thaw until just before it is cooked. Even if it is bought fresh, it will spoil very quickly unless kept under refrigeration. Thus more care must be taken with buying fish than other items. Also, there is no point in looking for "organic" fish. Some bodies of water are cleaner than others, but with fish it is best to take what is available nearby.

If you live near a port, send some members to talk with commercial fishermen and ask: if they will sell to you; their prices for the different kinds of fish they catch; if they gut, scale and behead the fish; and if they refrigerate the fish while they are out in the boat.

If you don't live near a port and still want to get fish cheaply for your conspiracy, go talk to the owners or managers of several of the local fish shops. Tell them what you are doing and ask who supplies their fish. You can then call the supplier to get wholesale prices. Some wholesalers have minimum orders of 25 pounds of each kind of fish. If this is too much for your conspiracy ask if the store manager will give you a discount price for regular quantity purchases. If you live near a large Chinese community, look in the Chinatown fish markets; it's usually cheaper and fresher here. This is especially true if you have a member who speaks the language of the proprietor. The coordinator should:
- Take orders and money, and add up how much of each fish is ordered.
- Make sure someone will pick up and pay for the fish. That person should have a leakproof box with ice in it with him when he gets the fish. (That smell you associate with fish is really rotting fish—fresh fish has no more smell than fresh beef or lamb.) The fish should be the last item picked up on a round of errands so that it will not rot or thaw.
- Make sure the fish stays refrigerated until members come to pick it up.
- Make sure each member gets what he paid for.

Fish/How to Eat It

PARMESAN SOUP

Put in a saucepan and heat
gently:
1 potato, chopped, soaked in
3 cups milk
salt and pepper to taste
1 pound fish, cut in bite-sized
    pieces (butterfish, halibut,
    cod)
Add to soup:
chopped garlic and chopped
    onions to taste
1/2 cup or more chopped
    parsley or celery leaves
Add, until soup has a cheese
flavor:
1/2 cup or more grated Parmesan
    cheese
Simmer gently until potato is
cooked. A few minutes before
serving, add:
chopped tomato
Ladle into bowls and sprinkle
with:
paprika
Serves 4

TANGY FISH SOUP

Wash and clean, removing head
and/or tail, and fins; then place
in Dutch oven or casserole:
1 whole white fish or fish fillets
Sprinkle fish well with:
paprika, salt and pepper
Place in cavity and on outside
of fish:
5 garlic cloves, chopped
Mix together and place over
and around fish:
2 tablespoons olive oil
1/3 cup sesame seeds
1/2 teaspoon dill weed
2 small potatoes, diced
3 celery stalks, chopped
Sprinkle well over everything:
paprika, salt and pepper
1 tablespoon sesame seeds
1 teaspoon minced parsley
Add to casserole:
3 quarts water
Bring water to boil, cover and
simmer 30 minutes. Turn fish
over and sprinkle on top:
1 tablespoon sesame seeds
1 tablespoon minced parsley
2 to 3 tomatoes, chopped
Simmer 15 to 30 minutes. Serve
with an additional sprinkling
of:
paprika (optional)
Serves 8 to 10

ANCHOVY TOMATO MARINADE

Arrange on a plate:
2 tomatoes, sliced
Mix together and pour over
tomatoes:
1/2 cup olive oil
1/4 cup wine vinegar
oregano and sweet basil to taste
1 garlic clove, minced
1 2-1/4-ounce can anchovy
    fillets, mashed
Sprinkle over top:
2 parsley sprigs, chopped
Refrigerate at least 30 minutes
before eating.
Serves 2 as a light lunch,
4 as a dinner salad

FISH KEDGEREE

Mix together:
2 cups hot cooked rice
2 cups cooked and flaked fish
4 hard-boiled eggs, chopped
1/2 cup cream or milk
1 teaspoon salt
several shakes cayenne pepper
Heat for several minutes over
low heat.
Serves 4

SALMON OR BONITA
SALAD SANDWICH

Mix together well:
1 7-ounce can salmon or bonita,
   flaked (cooked and flaked
   fresh fish may be substituted)
2 tablespoons mayonnaise
1/2 cup chopped olives
chopped chives to taste
1/8 to 1/4 teaspoon each garlic
   powder, coriander and ground
   ginger
1 parsley sprig, chopped
Serve on bread. This tastes best
if you use homemade
mayonnaise.
Serves 2 to 4

TUNA FISH
SALAD SANDWICH

Mix together well:
1 7-ounce can oil- or water-packed
   tuna, flaked
1 pickle, chopped
1 1-inch thick pineapple slice,
   chopped
1 heaping tablespoon
   mayonnaise (optional)
Spread mixture thickly on slices
of:
whole-wheat bread
Serves 2 to 4

LILLIAN'S WEST COAST
GEFILTE FISH

Fillet, reserving the heads:
1 pound red snapper
1 pound turbot or halibut
2 pounds fillet of sole
1 pound salmon
Run fillets through a meat
grinder with:
1 medium-sized onion
Add to fish and blend together
with a chopping blade in a
wooden bowl:
3 eggs
1/2 teaspoon salt
1/2 teaspoon cayenne or
   white pepper
1 tablespoon sugar
1 tablespoon matzo meal
   or matzo crumbs
Continue chopping and
gradually add:
1/2 cup water
Chop until well blended, about
5 minutes. Taste, adjust seasonings and let stand.
Place a trivet on the bottom of a
6- to 8-quart pot. Pare, slice and
place on the trivet:
1 large parsnip
1 large parsley root
2 carrots
2 large onions

Place on top of vegetables:
1 teaspoon salt
1 teaspoon white or cayenne
   pepper
2 fish heads
Cover ingredients in pot with
cold water and bring to a boil.
With wet hands, form balls with
the fish mixture and place them
in the gently boiling broth. (The
balls may be hamburger size,
meatball size or anything
in between.) Cover the pot and
cook, maintaining a gentle boil.
Check occasionally to make sure
that broth is surrounding the fish
balls at all times. Taste broth after
an hour and adjust seasonings.
When fish balls are cooked,
remove gently to a platter. Strain
the broth, reserving the vegetables,
and cool. Return the fish balls
to the broth while it cools so
that they absorb more flavor.
When balls are cool, refrigerate.
Serve fish balls with horseradish
and reserved vegetables as garnish.
The broth may be eaten as soup.
This recipe can be canned at
15 pounds pressure for 1 hour.

Fish/How to Eat It

FISH WITH RED SWEET AND SOUR SLURPY SAUCE

Deep fry, bake, steam or pressure cook until done:
4 pounds frozen or fresh fish, cut in serving pieces
Sauté:
1 onion, chopped, in
oil
To make sauce, combine:
1 cup vinegar
1 cup honey
1 cup tomato sauce
1 tablespoon tomato paste
the sautéed onion
1/2 to 1 cup raisins
1 tablespoon cinnamon
Mix together, add to sauce and heat to simmer:
3 cups water
3 tablespoons cornstarch
Place fish on rice or naked plate and pour heated sauce over it. Serve with peas and waterchestnuts.
Serves 8

ROLLED SOLE

Cook 2 to 3 minutes in oil:
1 large yellow onion, diced
4 carrots, very thinly sliced
6 to 8 parsley sprigs, chopped
1 tablespoon ground cumin (optional)
Add to pan:
enough water to cover bottom
Cover and simmer until carrots are tender. Add to vegetables and mix in thoroughly:
1/4 cup or more green chili peppers, sliced
salt and pepper to taste
Have ready:
6 fillets of sole
1-1/2 cups bread crumbs, wheat germ or soy grits
1 or 2 onions, sliced in rings (optional)
approximately 1 cup water
On each fillet, spread an equal amount of the cooked vegetables. Roll as tightly as possible and dip in bread crumbs and wheat germ or soy grits. Secure each roll with a toothpick and place in a baking dish on a bed of onions, if desired. Add water to a depth of 1/8 to 1/4 inch, cover with foil or a lid and bake at 400° for 30 minutes, or until fish is white.
Serves 3 to 4

FISH WITH TAHINI SAUCE

Cut crosswise into serving pieces:
1 2-pound fish
Sprinkle the cavities and the outsides of the fish with:
salt
Stuff the cavities with:
1 to 2 onions, sliced in rings
Fry the fish until well browned. Sprinkle while frying with:
cayenne pepper
powdered ginger
To make sauce, thin until it can be poured:
1 cup tahini
approximately 1/2 cup water
Mix into tahini:
1 to 2 garlic cloves, chopped
juice of 1 lemon
Pour sauce over fish, place in 350° oven and bake 20 minutes, or until tahini looks golden.
Serve hot with:
parsley
Serves 4

POLENTA ENOUGH
(Fish and Cornmeal Casserole)

Steam until carrots are tender:
1 carrot, thinly sliced
2 celery stalks, thinly chopped
1 pound potatoes, thinly sliced
Sauté lightly until white:
1-1/4 pounds butterfish or other
    white fish (approximately
    2 fillets)
In the bottom of a 2-1/2-quart
casserole, layer 1/4 inch deep:
approximately 1 cup cooked
    cornmeal mush
In the order given, layer half of
each of these ingredients on top
of the cornmeal:
the cooked vegetables
1/2 pound mushrooms, sliced
salt and pepper to taste
1/2 to 3/4 cup chopped parsley
the sautéed fish
Repeat layering with the remaining half of each of the ingredients.
Sprinkle on top:
1/4 cup cornmeal
Bake covered at 350° for about
30 minutes.
Serves 4

FISH FEAST

Wash and clean, removing head
and fins:
1 2-1/2- to 3-pound salmon with
    tail left on
Sprinkle inside and out with:
salt, pepper, minced garlic,
    rosemary, thyme, basil,
    oregano
In the bottom of a baking dish,
make a layer of:
2 onions, sliced in thin rings
Place fish on top of onions.
Arrange around the fish:
2 to 3 celery stalks, chopped
2 large carrots, sliced
Sprinkle on top:
1/2 cup chopped parsley
salt to taste
Add water to baking dish to a
depth of 1/2 inch and cover with
lid to prevent burning. Place fish
in a 450° to 500° oven until
water comes to a boil; lower heat
to 400° and bake 45 minutes.
Remove cover and bake for an
additional 10 to 15 minutes. This
fish is good served with rice or
potatoes. Or put some sliced
potatoes in the baking dish with
the fish. It looks nice garnished
with hard-boiled egg slices and
parsley.

HALIBUT HORN EYE

Sauté in oil until carrots are
tender:
4 carrots, thinly sliced
2 medium-sized yellow onions,
    diced
6 garlic cloves, minced
2 tablespoons or more sesame
    seeds
Add as needed to keep vegetables
from sticking:
1/2 to 3/4 cup stock, bouillon or
    water
Add to pan with vegetables:
4 halibut or other white fish
    fillets, cut in bite-sized pieces
salt and pepper to taste
Cook until fish is white and flaky
and serve with steamed potatoes.
To give this dish even more
flavor, marinate the fish in soy
sauce for 1 or 2 hours before
cooking.
Serves 4 to 6

Fish/How to Eat It

FISH CHUNKS AUX FINES HERBES

Have ready:
1-1/2 pounds fish of choice, cut
    in 1-inch or larger chunks
1 cup whole-wheat flour
Roll the fish chunks in the flour
and then sauté in:
butter or oil
When fish is almost done, add:
1 small onion, chopped, or
1 bunch green onions, chopped
1/2 to 3/4 cup chopped parsley
chervil and tarragon to taste
Add to pan and cook about
5 minutes more:
1/2 cup chopped mushrooms
1/4 to 1/2 cup white wine
1 teaspoon lemon juice
Serves 3

ALWAYS JUICY SALMON STEAKS

Sprinkle inside and out:
2 salmon steaks, with
salt
Combine in a bowl:
1/2 cup Tamari soy sauce
1/2 cup water
1 teaspoon ground ginger

Place fish in the marinade and let
stand 1 hour. Meanwhile, sauté
in a frying pan large enough to
hold the fish:
1 to 2 onions, chopped
Place the fish in the pan with the
sautéed onions and fry on both
sides until flaky. Be careful not
to overcook, as this fish becomes
dry.
Serves 2

TICKLE-TUMMIED FISH

Wash and clean, removing head,
tail and fins:
1 fish
Mix together:
1/2 cup cooked rice
1/2 cup raisins
salt, cayenne pepper and curry
    powder to taste
1 garlic clove, chopped
Stuff this mixture into fish
cavity. Place the fish on its back
and prop it up with:
2 medium-sized onions, quartered
Don't worry if the fish topples
off the onion quarters. Sprinkle
some water over the fish and
place in a 300° oven. Cook 40
minutes per pound.
Serves 2 per pound of fish

SALMON CAKE OR CAKES

Mix together:
1 16-ounce can salmon, flaked, or
1 pound cooked salmon with
    cooking liquid, flaked
1 to 1-1/2 cups cracker or bread
    crumbs
1 egg, beaten
salt and pepper to taste (optional)
Add to fish mixture to taste:
chopped olives
green pepper
celery and green onions (optional)
Shape fish mixture into patties
or loaf. Roll patties or loaf in:
1 cup cornmeal
Bake loaf at 375° to 400° until
browned or fry patties in oil
until browned.
Serves 2

Grains

Even though the percentage of savings is high when buying grains in bulk, the actual money savings is relatively low. A conspiracy can save its members as much as 30 to 50 percent on an item, but in actual dollar savings this may be only 5 to 15 cents per pound. The main reasons for buying grains in bulk are the opportunity to purchase unusual grains and the ability to control quality and freshness. Most conspiracies combine a grain run with honeys, oils, beans, nuts, seeds, dried fruits, herbs and spices into a bulk-goods run, because there are huge savings on these other items and many of them come from the same suppliers as the grains.

A typical bulk-foods family order will run $20. For this you will get enough food to fill up the back seat of a car or the arms of every member of your family. The food will smell so good that you will hardly be able to wait until you get home so you can pour your food into its waiting containers. Then you can smell, touch and taste each grain or fruit individually—the freshly ground whole-wheat flour, the delicious coconut flakes, the tangy dried apricots, the freshly shelled pecans, the toasted buckwheat groats, the cinnamon, nutmeg, thyme, sassafras and fenugreek. You'll dip your fingers into the honeys, molasses, soy sauce and maple syrup, and run your hands through the alfalfa seeds and garbanzo beans. The food will all be gone in a month or two and you'll be able to do it all over again.

The instructions for doing a bulk-goods run take up a lot of space, but the run itself is actually very easy.

FINDING SUPPLIERS Possible sources for grains include specialty bakers, bakery suppliers, restaurant suppliers, bean and elevator companies, organic farms like Wehah and Arrowhead Mills and health-food distributing companies like El Molino, Erewhon and Spiral Foods. To get the names of those nearest you, look in the yellow pages under the name of the grain you want, and under "grains" as well as the general topics given above. You should also ask your local health food and natural food stores where they get their food. (You will usually have to take your supplier's word for the "organicness" of his grains.) Look up specialty food companies, too, like Jewish food suppliers for buckwheat groats and Oriental food suppliers for white and brown rice and rice bran (nuka). Local Mormons may also have a supply house, as they keep a one-year's food allowance on hand at all times. Seventh Day Adventists may also have a stock of natural foods.

With grains you have almost no hope of finding one supplier who can meet all your needs. Nobody carries all the items you will want and everybody is frequently out of stock on some items. If you find many suppliers you will have to keep careful track of who has which items at what prices. It is a good idea to make a chart with the items you want listed down the side and the names of the suppliers going across the top. In the squares, you should put the price per pound for each item and the units in which it is available.

Prices on grains are not steady; they vary with each new crop and the price goes up towards the end of the season when supplies are getting low. When you are dealing in fluctuating prices with a lot of suppliers, you will need careful bookkeeping, too, to keep you from spending more than you take in.

DOING GRAINS

When you find out what foods are available in your area, make a list of all of them and their prices. Show this list to the members. From these foods, members should choose a limited number for the ordering list, so that reasonable quantities of what is listed can be bought. For example, some members might prefer long-grain brown rice over short-grain brown rice, but would take the short-grain rice if the long-grain rice wasn't listed. The more members you have, the greater variety of items you will be able to list. After you have decided which items to list, members can make individual copies of the order form or copies could be run off on a ditto machine if you have access to one. (For a sample form see page 135.) To order grains a conspiracy will need:

- A list of items available and their approximate prices.
- A members' sign-up list for order collators, telephoners, drivers, baggers and clean-up duty. The drivers' list should indicate which suppliers are on which route, so the members can pick which territory they want to cover. In a small conspiracy, one person could be the collator and telephoner. You would only need one driver, and the baggers could do cleanup.
- Scales for weighing out individual orders (these should be accurate within an ounce).

- Bags for bagging individual orders, as well as empty clean jars and bottles for peanut butter, honey and oil.
- Marking pens for writing names and amounts on bags and tape for holding bags shut.
- A place to do the bagging. (Many churches will loan you a basement or room.)
    In order for the whole operation to go smoothly, members will also need:
- To pay for the food at the same time as placing the orders.
- To put in 10 minutes work for each item they order, whether it be as collators, telephoners, drivers, baggers or for cleaning up.
- To provide bags, a cardboard box, and clean bottles or jars for the items they order. (Do not write names on the bags. It is really confusing to try to hunt down someone's bag when filling an order. If you really want your honey put in a special jar, the baggers can probably handle it.)
- To pay a five percent markup to cover gas, bridge tolls, telephone toll calls, marking pens, masking tape, and the inevitable spills and extras. Some conspiracies include in the markup the cost of buying new bags wholesale. Doing grain requires a big supply of bags and very often second-hand bags have holes in them which could mean the loss of a member's order of grain unless you tape them up before filling them. A large new bag costs 2 to 3 cents.

COLLATING ORDERS

The collator should have separate pieces of paper at least three by five inches for each item on the list. The name of an item should be on one side of the card and the names of the people ordering that item and the amount they want should be written on the other side. (Sample below.) The collator need only add up the numbers on the card to get the total ordered. Most bulk suppliers sell food only in multiples of five pounds. Some sell 5-, 10-, 25-, 50- and 100-pound sacks with lower prices per pound for the larger sacks. When the collator adds up your members' orders, there will probably be totals like 17 pounds carob powder and 73 pounds whole-wheat flour. If carob comes in 5-, 10- and 25-pound sacks, the collator must

```
organic whole wheat flour

.12/lb
```

side 1

```
Mary  10      Katy 8
Anna   5      Tony 5     order: 50 lb.
David 15      _____
Eric  13       46 lb.    extra: 4 lb
```

side 2

decide whether to buy 15 pounds and short the two highest orders by one pound each, buy 20 pounds and have three pounds extra, or buy 25 pounds and get a lower price but have eight pounds extra. The answer will depend on the price break the quantity purchase will get, the amount of money you have from markups, and your members' appetites. If your members are impulse buyers who will try some carob powder just because it is there, the collator will have a bit more leeway in purchasing than he would if they are very poor or are unwilling to try new things. The collator should indicate his decisions on the cards by either writing down "extra 2 pounds" or by drawing a line through an order that is to be shorted and writing in the new amount that will actually be bagged for that order. He should also write the total that will be ordered onto the card. These cards can then be used by the telephoners as they place the orders and by the baggers to check off each person's order as they fill it.

The telephoner should now call all the suppliers to check the prices and place the orders. It is his job to get as much as possible of the ordered food at as close as possible to the price on the conspiracy order list. He must use judgement. If millet was listed at 20 cents and it is now 25 cents per pound, should he buy it? The difference is only 5 cents per pound but it is a 25 percent increase. The answer will depend on your members, the buyer's mood and the store price you are trying to undersell. There will always be a few items that are out of stock, out of season or outrageously priced. The money that was collected for them can be used for stockpiling items selling at good prices that the members would probably buy. You must always keep in mind, however, that members who ordered unpurchased items will want their money back.

BUYING

When placing the order, the telephoner should inquire about possible discounts for paying cash and picking up the orders. He should ask that the food be ready one week from the date he is calling. He then should tell the drivers the pickup date and prepare for each of them a list of their pickup stops, showing the quantity and price of the items ordered from each supplier, plus the total owed each supplier. It is helpful also, if he gives them maps for their route.

Drivers should have the money or a check to pay for the food when it is picked up; the suppliers will be pleased, you might earn a discount and you will keep your books balanced. The drivers should compare the quantity and price of each item with the shopping list given him by the telephoner, before he pays the bill. After the run, he should give all invoices and receipts to the collator. The bagging should be

**DRIVING
FOR PICKUPS**

done the evening after the food is picked up or the next day. Anything that rots quickly like wheat germ should be refrigerated. The drivers should be willing to store the non-perishable grains in their cars until bagging time, unless the owners of your bagging room will let your group store them there.

BAGGING The first impulse of most novice baggers is to fill one member's order completely and then start on another's. This works fine if you have only two members to deal with. Usually though, in order to make sure the weighing is accurate, you must first compare the total amount ordered by all the members with the amount on hand and figure out what compensation is to be made, if any. Then you should weigh each item out for all the members who ordered it before going on to the next item. For example you should weigh out all the barley before going on to the cornmeal. Baggers should:

• Tape each person's order to the wall in alphabetical order and place a cardboard box under it to hold all the food.

• Take a card from the item deck, find the appropriate sack and take them to a scale.

• Write the name of the owner and the name and amount of the food in each bag or bottle onto the container immediately after filling it.

• Fold the bag shut; if it won't stay shut, tape it shut.

• Put each bag into its owner's box and put the extra, if any, into the extras pile.

• Check off the items on the order sheets as they are put into the boxes. Baggers should also mark any amount changes onto the order forms, so the bill calculator, who is also the collator, will know exactly what to charge each member.

Because you can get lower prices with greater volume, you might want to combine orders with other conspiracies in your area. If there are a great many people ordering, you should have a two-level bagging. At the first bagging, you would sort out the food by conspiracy, and at the second, each conspiracy would proceed as outlined above.

Grains, too, are a good source of protein. Popcorn, long touted as a "garbage food" is 12 percent protein according to the U.S. Department of Agriculture Handbook #8 (available from the government printing office in Washington D.C. for $2). Buckwheat is 11.7 percent, whole wheat is 14 percent and millet is 9.9 percent protein.

Grains/How to Eat It

HOW TO COOK WILD RICE

Have ready:
1/2 cup wild rice
1-1/2 to 2 cups water
Place rice into a saucepan and pour water over to a depth of 3 to 4 times as high as the wild rice. Bring water to a boil and continue cooking with or without a cover for 30 to 45 minutes. Drain and serve with salt. You will appreciate the unique flavor of the wild rice more and save on cost if you mix it with some brown rice for contrast.

HOW TO COOK MOST GRAINS

Place in a 2-quart pot with a tight-fitting lid and boil gently until done:
1 cup grain of choice
2 cups water
Cooking time varies with each grain. It can be 10 to 15 minutes for bulgur or about 40 minutes for brown rice. Every stove, pan and climate is different, so watch the grain carefully while it cooks.

YELLOW RICE

Combine in saucepan, bring to boil and cook covered over low heat until rice is done:
1 cup brown rice
2 cups chicken bouillon
1 tablespoon or more sesame seeds
1 teaspoon turmeric
1/2 to 3/4 cup raisins
1/4 to 1/2 cup chopped parsley
While rice is cooking, simmer together in a pan:
1 large onion, chopped
2 to 4 garlic cloves, minced
2 medium-sized carrots, sliced
1 celery stalk with leaves, chopped
approximately 1/4 cup water
Simmer until carrots are tender. When the rice is cooked, mix in:
the cooked vegetables
1/2 cup cashews (optional)
Serves 4

TO COOK BUCKWHEAT GROATS

Method 1
Have ready:
1 cup toasted groats
1 egg
Coat the groats with the egg by placing them both in a bowl and stirring well. Place the groats in a dry frying pan over low heat and push them around the pan with a spatula until they separate, indicating that the egg has cooked. Pour over the groats:
2 cups boiling water
Cover with a tight-fitting lid and cook about 20 minutes. Salt and serve.

Method 2
Have ready:
1 cup toasted groats
2 cups boiling water or stock
Add groats slowly to water or stock, stirring constantly (don't let the water stop boiling). Cover with a tight-fitting lid, lower heat and cook for 15 minutes.
Serves 2 to 3

SWEET AND SOUR BUCKWHEAT GROATS

Sauté:
1 large onion, chopped
1 to 3 garlic cloves, minced
oil
Add to frying pan and simmer:
3 tablespoons whole-wheat flour
1-1/2 teaspoons or less salt
3 tablespoons molasses
3 tablespoons apple cider
Add and cook until celery is tender:
3 tablespoons sesame seeds
2 celery stalks with leaves, chopped
2 tomatoes, chopped
3/4 cup chopped parsley
Mix into frying pan 2 minutes before removing from heat:
3/4 cup cashews (optional)
Serve over cooked buckwheat groats.

Variations
This is a very versatile recipe. It can also be served over rice, lentils or noodles. There are also many good vegetable substitutions, some of which are given here.
• Onion, celery, garlic, green peppers and tomatoes over lentils.
• Cauliflower, chopped bite-size, garlic, onion, parsley and cashews over rice.
• Green onions, 1/4 pound sprouts, celery, garlic, sesame seeds, apple chunks and cashews over millet.
• Pineapple, raisins, onion, sliced carrots, cashews and cinnamon over rice.
Serves 2 to 3

HOW TO COOK MILLET

Sauté until browned:
1 cup hulled millet, in
2 teaspoons oil
Pour over millet:
4 cups boiling water
Add:
1/4 teaspoon salt
1 onion, chopped (optional)
Cover pan and cook for about 30 minutes.

ASIAN BUCKWHEAT NOODLES

Bring to a boil in a 2-quart pot:
4 cups water
1 teaspoon salt
Add to pot:
1 teaspoon oil (optional)
1 to 2 cups buckwheat noodles
Noodles are cooked if they break easily when pushed against the side of the pot with a spoon. Drain noodles and save cooking water if you are making soup soon. Stir into cooked noodles:
1 green onion, sliced
To Make Sauce:
Mix together in a small bowl:
1/2 cup Tamari soy sauce
1 egg
1/4 teaspoon powdered ginger or shredded fresh ginger
This sauce may be poured cold or heated over the noodles.
Serves 2

Grains/How to Eat It

SPAETZLE
(Traditional South German Homemade Noodle)

Break into a bowl:
1 egg
Add to egg, stirring to make a smooth dough:
1 cup flour
1/2 teaspoon salt
Add to make dough into a heavy batter:
water, as needed
Bring to a boil:
3 quarts water
1 tablespoon salt
Dip a small cutting board into the boiling water. Place about 1/3 of the batter on the board and cut strips of the batter off the edge of the board, letting the knife enter the boiling water each time you make a cut. The spaetzle are cooked when they float. Remove the cooked spaetzle with a skimmer and store in a warm bowl until served. Continue cutting the spaetzle until all the batter is used.
Serves 2 to 3

MAMALIGA

Mix together well:
1 scant cup cornmeal
1-1/4 cups cold water
1 teaspoon salt
Slowly pour cornmeal mixture into:
2-3/4 cups boiling water
Boil for 2 to 3 minutes, then turn down the heat and simmer for about 15 minutes, or until mamaliga leaves the sides of the pan.
Add, mixing in until blended:
2 cups feta or other cheese, crumbled, or yogurt or sour cream
2 to 3 tablespoons butter
Serve as cornmeal pudding; fruit is a good accompaniment.
Serves 4 to 6

SELINA'S HIGH-PROTEIN PANCAKES

Beat until frothy:
8 eggs
Add to the eggs and beat again briefly:
2 cups water
Add through a sifter, slowly beating after each addition:
1-3/4 cups powdered milk
1-1/2 cups unbleached white flour
Then add, beating until smooth:
2 tablespoons safflower oil
1 tablespoon vanilla extract
Batter will be very thin. Using a large frying pan, pancake pan or skillet, heat pan to medium hot, greasing it with:
margarine or butter, or sweet butter for a restricted sodium diet
Pour batter into the center of the pan with a soup ladle and tip pan to spread, making a single, pan-sized pancake. The amount of batter you use depends on the size of the pan and your dexterity in flipping the pancake. See how thin you can make them. If you can't flip the pancakes without tearing them, add to the batter to thicken:
2 additional tablespoons flour
Serve Russian style with sour cream and jam, or with applesauce or plain.
Serves 5 to 6

OATMEAL WHATEVERS

Cook together in a covered pot until the oatmeal absorbs most of the water, about 10 minutes:
1 cup oatmeal
2 scant cups water
Pour the cooked oatmeal over:
1 medium-sized yellow onion, finely chopped
1 teaspoon mixed minced herbs (parsley, thyme, basil, etc.)
salt and cayenne pepper to taste
1 tablespoon tomato sauce (optional)
Add to oatmeal and mix to make a stiff dough, adding more bread crumbs if necessary:
1 egg, well beaten
minced parsley to taste
approximately 1/2 cup bread crumbs
Flour your hands and roll pieces of the dough into finger lengths. Fry them until done and serve with soy or taco sauce.
Makes approximately 2 dozen

PIE CRUST

Sift together:
2 cups flour
dash salt
Cut into flour with 2 knives or a pastry cutter until it looks the size of peas:
3/4 cup butter
Add, stirring with fork to mix in:
a dribble of honey
1 egg yolk
2 tablespoons brandy (optional)
Add, if needed to hold dough together:
1 tablespoon water
Form into ball, cover with plastic wrap and refrigerate 20 minutes before using. Makes a 2-crust 9- or 10-inch pie. For prebaked shell, bake at 350° 10 minutes. Left-over dough may be frozen.

ONION PIE AGAIN

To Make Crust:
Mix together thoroughly:
1/3 cup each rye flour, cornmeal and wheat germ
1/4 teaspoon salt
2/3 cup butter, softened
approximately 6 tablespoons hot water
Pat the dough into a large pie pan.

To Make Filling:
Sauté:
2 small red onions, chopped
1 large yellow onion, chopped
2 tablespoons butter
Sprinkle on sautéing onions:
1/4 teaspoon cayenne pepper
1/4 teaspoon salt
Drain the onions on paper towels.
Mix together and reserve to pour on top of pie:
1/3 cup honey
2 eggs, beaten
1/3 cup yogurt
1 cup milk
1/4 teaspoon nutmeg
dash salt
Place in the pie shell alternating layers of:
the sautéed onions
1-1/2 to 2 cups grated cheese of choice
Pour over the layered pie the reserved custard mixture.
Bake at 450° for 15 minutes. Then lower the oven temperature to 350° and bake until custard is done.
Serves 6 to 8

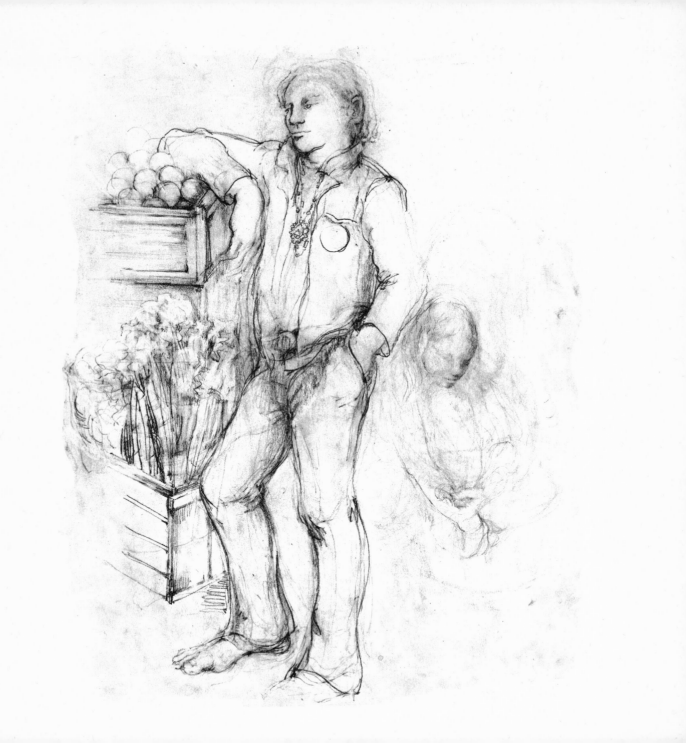

PUMPKIN BREAD

Mix together thoroughly:
2/3 cup butter, softened
2-2/3 cups raw sugar, or
approximately 2-1/3 cups honey
Mix into butter-sugar mixture:
4 eggs, beaten
2 cups cooked and puréed
   pumpkin
2/3 cup water
Sift together, then add to
pumpkin mixture:
3-1/3 cups whole-wheat flour
1/2 teaspoon baking soda
2 teaspoons baking powder
1-1/2 teaspoons salt
1 teaspoon or more cinnamon
1 teaspoon or more ground
   cloves
Stir into batter:
2/3 cup raisins
2/3 cup coarsely chopped
   walnuts
Pour into 2 greased loaf pans and
bake at 350° for 1 hour, or
until knife inserted in the middle
comes out clean.
Makes 2 loaves

CORNBREAD

Place in a bowl and stir until
well blended:
1 cup cornmeal
1 cup whole-wheat flour
2 teaspoons baking powder
1 teaspoon salt
1/3 cup oil
1 cup milk
1 egg
2 to 3 tablespoons honey
1 carrot, grated (optional)
Pour the batter into a buttered
8-inch square 2-inch deep pan
and bake at 400° for 25 minutes.
To serve, cut into 2-inch squares.
Makes 16 squares

OATMEAL BREAD
(First Prize Winner at the
"Little Farm Fair" in Berkeley)

Have ready:
2 cups oatmeal
2 tablespoons safflower oil
4 cups boiling water
Pour the boiling water over the
oatmeal and oil and let stand for
1 hour. Dissolve:
2 tablespoons active dry yeast, in
1/2 cup warm water

Let stand 5 minutes and combine
with oatmeal. Add and beat well,
using a mixer if desired when
adding the first 3 cups of flour:
1/3 cup honey
1/3 cup blackstrap molasses
1 tablespoon salt
approximately 9 to 10 cups
   whole-wheat flour
The flour should be added only
until the dough starts to come
clean from the sides of the bowl.
Turn the dough out onto a
heavily floured surface and knead
5 minutes, adding more flour if
necessary. Place the dough into a
greased bowl and let rise in a
warm place about 1-1/2 hours,
or until double in bulk. Punch
down, knead and let rise again,
about 45 minutes. Punch down
again, knead and shape into 3
loaves. Place in greased and
floured pans, let rise 20 minutes
and bake at 350° for 50 to 60
minutes.
Makes 3 loaves

Grains/How to Eat It

CRISS' CRUNCHY CAROB BREAD

Mix together and let stand for 10 minutes while the yeast softens and grows:
1 tablespoon active dry yeast
1/2 cup warm water
1 tablespoon honey
Add to yeast mixture:
1 scant tablespoon salt
1 cup lukewarm water
4 cups whole-wheat flour
1 cup carob flour
1/2 cup granola or familia
1/4 cup honey
Let rise until double in bulk, punch down and turn out on floured surface. Knead, adding more flour if necessary, and shape into a loaf. Place in a greased loaf pan in a warm place to rise 1-1/2 times its original size. Bake at 350° for 50 to 60 minutes.
Makes 1 large or 2 small loaves

IDA'S CRANBERRY-NUT BREAD

Sift together:
2 cups whole-wheat or unbleached white flour
1/2 teaspoon each salt and baking soda
1-1/2 teaspoons baking powder
Combine with dry ingredients:
1 egg, beaten
2 tablespoons oil or melted butter
1/2 cup orange juice
2 teaspoons hot water
Mix into batter:
1/2 cup chopped walnuts
1 cup chopped cranberries
Bake at 325° for 1 hour and 10 minutes. Brush with melted butter, wrap in wax paper while still hot and place in the refrigerator for 3 hours. Remove paper, wrap in towel and return to refrigerator until ready to eat.
Makes 1 loaf

ARABIC POCKET BREAD

Mix together and let stand until foamy, about 10 minutes:
1 tablespoon active dry yeast
1/2 cup warm water
1 teaspoon honey
Mix into yeast and let stand until the mixture looks like a sponge and has doubled in bulk:
1 cup warm water
1 scant tablespoon salt
2-1/2 cups whole-wheat flour
Add to dough, until it is no longer sticky:
1-1/2 cups or more whole-wheat flour
Knead dough and then let stand in warm place to rise for about 1 hour. Break dough in about 16 pieces. Roll each piece out into a 1/8-inch-thick circle. Let the circles rise about 45 minutes, or until they look dimpled on the top and bottom. Turn the pita over if the tops start to dry out. Bake in a preheated 500° oven until done, 10 to 15 minutes. When done, the pita is hollow in the middle, like a pocket. Four out of 5 usually work. They should be left in the oven long enough so they don't collapse, but not too long so they don't get hard. Fill with humous (page 106), tahini (page 115) or felafel (page 110).
Makes 16

HEALTH BRAN

Mix together well:
4 cups bran
2 cups whole-wheat flour
1 teaspoon baking soda
1 teaspoon salt
Add to flour mixture and combine thoroughly:
2-1/2 cups buttermilk
2 tablespoons dark molasses
Place in 2 small greased loaf pans and bake at 275° for 1 hour.
Makes 2 loaves

NUTTY BANANA BREAD

Place in a bowl and beat together until well blended:
2 cups whole-wheat flour
1/2 teaspoon each baking powder, baking soda and salt
4 tablespoons butter or oil
1/2 cup brown sugar, or
1/4 cup honey
1/4 cup powdered milk
1 egg, beaten
2 or 3 very-ripe bananas, mashed
3 tablespoons milk, soured with lemon juice
1/2 cup chopped walnuts or pecans
Put in a well-buttered loaf pan and bake at 350° for 50 to 60 minutes.
Makes 1 loaf

KULICH

Dissolve:
2 tablespoons active dry yeast, in
1/2 cup lukewarm water
Cream together:
1/3 cup sugar
1/4 pound butter
Add to creamed mixture:
1-1/2 cups milk, scalded and cooled
3 cups flour
2 to 3 teaspoons salt
Combine mixture with dissolved yeast. Cover dough with greased wax paper and a cloth and let rise. Meanwhile, mix together thoroughly:
1 cup butter, softened
2 cups sugar
Then add:
2 whole eggs
5 egg yolks
almond flavoring to taste
vanilla extract to taste
grated rind of 1 lemon
6 to 8 ounces almond paste, broken up
Place dough on floured cloth or board. Add to the risen dough alternately, a little at a time, the egg batter and:
5 to 6 cups flour

Keep a ring of flour along the outside and use a long spatula to handle the mixing when the dough gets too sticky. When thoroughly combined, mix into the dough:
3-1/4 cups mixed fruit peels, finely shredded
1/2 cup raisins (optional)
3/4 cup blanched almonds, ground or slivered (optional)
(To blanch the almonds, pour boiling water over the shelled nuts and let stand until skins can be slipped off.) If you find yourself tiring of the kneading, work small sections of the dough at a time. Fill cans (28-ounce or 46-ounce-size cans work best; be sure the cans have no bumps or ridges in them), that have been well greased, about half full. Let rise in cans until double in bulk. Bake at 375° to 400° about 45 to 50 minutes, depending on the thickness and diameter of the can. Be sure to grease the insides of the cans evenly or you will have to cut off the bottoms to remove the kulich without damaging it.
Makes approximately 3 loaves

Grains/How to Eat It

MATZOS

For Passover night, matzos should contain only water and flour. After all, if you had to make bread in a hurry, you wouldn't go out and milk the cow and get eggs from the chickens. For regular eating, the following recipe tastes good. You wouldn't mind eating it for a week straight. (This recipe works with just the flour and water.)

Mix together in a bowl, adding the flour until mixture is dough-like:

1-1/2 cups water or milk
approximately 4-1/2 cups whole-wheat, barley or oat flour
2 teaspoons salt
1 egg
1/3 cup butter or oil (optional)
1 cup yogurt, mixed with
1/4 cup honey (optional)

Break off a fist-sized piece of dough and place it on a floured board or pastry cloth. Roll out as thin as possible with a floured rolling pin. Repeat with remaining dough and bake at 400° for about 15 minutes.
Makes 16 to 20

BUTTERHORN ROLLS

Place in a bowl and let yeast grow until foamy:

1 tablespoon active dry yeast
1/4 cup warm water or milk
1 teaspoon honey

Add to yeast to make a workable dough:

1 rounded teaspoon salt
approximately 4 cups whole-wheat flour
1/4 cup nutritional yeast, or an additional 1/4 cup whole-wheat flour
1/2 cup oil
1/4 cup honey or brown sugar
3 large eggs
1 cup milk

Knead dough until it is firm and elastic and roll out in a circle about 1/4 inch thick. Cut the circle into pie-like sections and roll each section into a curl, starting with the wide end. Let the curls rise until double in bulk and bake on an ungreased cookie sheet at 400° for 18 to 20 minutes. This dough also makes good bread. Just form into a loaf, put in a greased loaf pan and bake at 350° for 50 to 60 minutes.
Makes 16 to 24

FRUIT POPOVERS

Mix together thoroughly:

1 cup whole-wheat flour
1 cup milk
1 or more eggs
pinch salt

Heat a buttered muffin pan in a very hot oven until it hisses when you throw water at it. Fill each muffin cup slightly over halfway full with the batter.
Have ready:

1 banana, sliced, or
1/2 to 3/4 cup blueberries or fruit of choice

Place a slice of banana or several blueberries on top of each popover and bake at 450° for 30 minutes. Lower temperature to 350° and bake for 15 minutes.
Makes 12

RORO'S SCHNECKEN

Place in a cup:
1 tablespoon active dry yeast
1/4 teaspoon salt
1/2 teaspoon honey or sugar
Scald:
1 cup milk
Allow milk to cool slightly and pour 1/4 cup of it on the yeast. Stir to help the yeast grow. Save the remaining milk for later. Put in a large bowl and stir together:
1/4 pound butter, at room temperature, or
1/2 cup oil plus 1/2 teaspoon salt
1/2 cup honey or sugar
2 eggs, slightly beaten
3-1/2 cups flour
1/2 teaspoon salt
Add to the flour mixture:
the softened yeast
the 3/4 cup reserved milk
Now, this is the hard part. Beat by hand with a wooden spoon until the dough leaves the sides of the bowl, about 15 minutes. This is to get air into the dough and make it light. An electric mixer will do the job, but the final product will not be as good. If you are tired now, you can put some plastic wrap over the bowl and put it in the refrigerator overnight where it will rise slowly. Or, let it rise right now until it doubles in bulk. If you refrigerate the dough, let it reach room temperature before working with it. Prepare the muffin tins by melting over low heat:
1/2 pound butter
Place 1 scant tablespoon of the butter into each of 24 muffin cups. Place on top of butter, flat side up:
24 pecan halves
Soften, heating in a saucepan if necessary:
1-1/2 cups brown sugar, mixed with
2 tablespoons water
Place 1 tablespoon of the sugar into each muffin cup.
Roll out 1/3 of the dough on a floured cloth or board in a 12x18-inch rectangle 1/4 inch thick. Brush the dough with:
oil or melted butter
Then sprinkle with a mixture of:
brown sugar and cinnamon
Top with a generous sprinkling of:
chopped pecans
raisins or currants
Roll the dough from the long side like a newspaper. Cut in 8 1-1/2-inch pieces and place each piece, cut side up, on top of the butter, pecan and sugar in the muffin cup. Repeat with remaining dough. Allow to rise in cups until double in bulk.

Bake at 375° for about 15 minutes. Turn out immediately onto wax paper. The easiest way to do this is to put the wax paper on a cookie sheet, put the cookie sheet, wax paper side down, on the schnecken and turn the pans upside down. This will make the butter and sugar dribble down the sides of the schnecken. Let cool and freeze to bring out the best flavor; warm up before serving. This recipe is a lot of work so make a big batch.
Makes 24
This recipe requires longer cooking time at altitudes over 5000 feet—about 7 minutes extra.

PINEAPPLE MUFFINS

Stir together:
1 cup sifted flour
3/4 teaspoon salt
2-1/4 teaspoons baking powder
1/4 teaspoon cinnamon
1/2 teaspoon cracked wheat
1/4 cup wheat germ
1/3 cup brown sugar
1 egg
1 cup crushed pineapple
1/3 cup vegetable oil
Fill greased muffin tins two-thirds full and bake 20 to 25 minutes at 375°.

HOW TO MAKE SOURDOUGH STARTER

Have clean and ready:
a 2-quart nonmetal container
Place into container:
**1 tablespoon active dry yeast, or
    1 fresh yeast cake**
1/2 cup warm water
Add to container and mix in well:
**2 tablespoons honey or brown
    sugar**
Add and stir in well:
2-1/4 cups whole-wheat flour
**1/4 cup sesame meal (pulver-
    ized raw sesame seeds), or**
**an additional 1/4 cup whole-
    wheat flour**
Add and mix all ingredients together well:
2 cups warm water
Cover the container with a wet cloth secured with a rubberband. Let this mixture stand on your kitchen counter to ferment for 5 days. Be sure to shake or beat it down once a day. Stirring with a spoon usually does it.
On the fifth day beat in:
1/4 cup whole-wheat flour
1/4 cup warm water

Place the starter in the refrigerator. Beat your starter every day. It will separate and stop fermenting if you forget for too many days in a row. When you use the starter replace every cup you take with 1 cup flour (with or without sesame meal in it) and 1 cup warm water. If you don't use the starter for over a week, add 1/4 cup flour and 1/4 cup water to it to keep it happy. If it stops smelling winy, throw it out. Throw it out once a year anyway, just to start over with fresh ingredients and a clean container. If you know you aren't going to use the starter for a while, it may be frozen; just remember to feed it as soon as it is thawed. It is this starter plus 1 tablespoon vinegar per cup of starter that gives French bread its flavor. For very sour bread put the starter, vinegar, salt and some flour into a bowl, mix well and pour about 1/3 cup warm water over them; don't mix in the water. Cover the whole thing with a damp cloth and let stand overnight. Make the bread in the morning.

SOURDOUGH CHOCOLATE CAKE

Mix together:
1 cup starter (preceding recipe)
3/4 cup honey
1/2 cup oil or butter
2 eggs
1 cup milk
1 teaspoon vanilla extract
rounded 1/2 cup cocoa powder
1-1/2 teaspoons baking soda
1/2 teaspoon salt
2 cups whole-wheat flour
Pour in buttered cake pans and bake for 30 to 40 minutes in a preheated 350° oven. Serve without frosting; it is very moist and sweet.
Serves 8 to 10

SUPER ICING

Sift together:
1-1/4 cups powdered sugar
1-1/4 cups powdered milk
Beat into sifted ingredients:
4 tablespoons butter, softened
1/2 cup evaporated milk
1 teaspoon vanilla extract
dash salt
Add a little more evaporated milk or powdered milk to adjust consistency to taste.
Ices a 2-layer cake

MRS. CURTO'S BANANA CAKE COMES TO BERKELEY
(First Prize Winner at the "Little Farm Fair" in Berkeley)

Mix together in a 4-quart bowl:
1/4 pound butter, softened
1-1/2 cups brown sugar
1 teaspoon vanilla extract
3 egg yolks
1/2 cup chopped nuts
Add to bowl and mix in:
1 cup mashed bananas
    (2 to 3 ripe bananas)
1 teaspoon salt
1 teaspoon baking powder
1 teaspoon baking soda
Add alternately, in small amounts, stirring after each addition:
2 cups whole-wheat pastry flour
1/2 cup buttermilk or
    milk soured with lemon juice
Beat until stiff and fold in:
3 egg whites
Pour batter in 2 greased 8-inch round cake pans. Bake at 350° for 40 to 45 minutes. Ice with super icing (page 97).
Serves 8

MOTHER TRUCKER'S STRANGE CAKES
(With Tahini-Honey Frosting)

Blend together in a large bowl:
1/4 cup oil
1 cup raw sugar, or
slightly less honey
Add to bowl and blend in well, adding dry ingredients alternately with the liquid:
2 eggs, beaten
2 cups less 3 tablespoons
    whole-wheat or unbleached
    white flour
3 tablespoons soy flour
1/4 teaspoon salt
2-1/2 teaspoons baking powder
3/4 cup milk
1 teaspoon vanilla (optional)
Pour into greased 8-inch square pan and bake at 350° for about 35 minutes, or until a knife inserted in center comes out clean.
To Make Frosting:
Mix and spread on cake just before eating:
1/2 cup sesame tahini
1/2 cup honey

STRANGE CAKE VARIATIONS

Peanut butter cake:
Add 1/2 cup peanut butter to recipe and substitute peanut butter for sesame tahini in frosting, if desired.
Spice cake:
Add 1 teaspoon cinnamon, 1 teaspoon allspice, 1/4 teaspoon powdered ginger, 1/4 teaspoon cardamom and 3/4 cup raisins.
Fruit cake:
Place sliced apples and/or peaches in pan before pouring in batter. Place some slices on top also; glaze top with honey and sprinkle with sugar and/or cinnamon.
This recipe can also be used to make cupcakes, or you can add nuts, raisins, sunflower seeds, fruit, berries or anything and everything else.

TOMATO SOUP CAKE

Cream together in a 3-quart bowl:
1/4 pound butter, softened
1 cup sugar
1 egg, beaten
Dissolve:
1 teaspoon baking soda, in
1 can condensed tomato soup
Sift together and add alternately with soup to creamed mixture:
1-3/4 cups flour
2 teaspoons ground cloves
1 teaspoon cinnamon
1/2 teaspoon nutmeg
1/8 teaspoon salt
Stir until thoroughly mixed and then fold in:
1 cup ground raisins or sliced dates
1 cup chopped walnuts
Bake in a greased loaf pan at 350° for 45 to 55 minutes. Frost with cream cheese frosting. Use homemade soup if you want, but don't miss out on a good cake.

JEAN'S WHOLE-WHEAT ORANGE CAKE

Sift together:
1 cup whole-wheat flour
2 teaspoons baking powder
Mix together, then combine with sifted ingredients:
4 tablespoons butter, softened
1/2 cup sugar
3 eggs
3/4 cup milk
Add to batter and stir in well:
grated rind of 1 orange
1/2 teaspoon vanilla
Bake at 350° 20 minutes, or until toothpick inserted in center comes out clean.

IRENE'S APPLE CAKE

Stir together in a large bowl:
1 cup unbleached flour
1 teaspoon cinnamon
1 teaspoon baking soda
1/2 teaspoon salt
2 or 3 eggs, unbeaten
1/2 cup safflower oil
Add to bowl and stir in:
4 apples, unpeeled, cored and chopped
1 cup sugar, or
1/2 cup honey
1 cup washed raisins
1 cup chopped walnuts
1 cup wheat germ
Pour into ungreased metal loaf pan and bake for 1 hour at 350°. Cool in pan, then remove.

MEXICAN WEDDING COOKIES

Mix together and beat well:
2 cups whole-wheat flour
1 cup ground walnuts
1 cup butter
4 tablespoons powdered sugar
1 teaspoon vanilla extract
Form into walnut-sized balls and bake 15 minutes at 325°. Roll, coating lightly, in:
1/2 cup powdered sugar
Makes 2 dozen

Grains/How to Eat It

PERSIMMON COOKIES

Cream together:
1/4 pound butter, softened
2 whole eggs, beaten, or
4 egg yolks, beaten
1 cup brown sugar
Combine:
2 cups whole-wheat flour
1 teaspoon baking soda
1/2 teaspoon ground cloves
1/2 teaspoon cinnamon
1 teaspoon nutmeg
Combine the creamed mixture with the dry ingredients and add:
1 cup persimmon pulp
1 cup chopped walnuts
1 cup raisins
Drop by spoonfuls onto greased cookie sheets and bake at 350° for 8 to 10 minutes, or until golden brown.
Makes approximately 4 dozen

GINGER-VANILLA CURLS

Heat until boiling:
1/2 cup blackstrap molasses
Add and stir until melted:
1/4 pound butter, or
1/2 cup oil
Add gradually, stirring constantly:
1-1/8 cups whole-wheat flour
1/4 teaspoon salt
2/3 cup brown sugar
1 tablespoon powdered ginger
3 tablespoons vanilla extract
When batter is smooth, drop by 1/2 teaspoonfuls 3 inches apart (9 to 12 at a time) onto a well-buttered cookie sheet. Bake at 300° for 10 minutes. Remove from oven and let cool for 1 minute. Lift from pan with a spatula. The cookie will mash together if you try to lift it too early; it will stick to the pan if you try too late. (If this happens, just stick the pan back into the oven for a minute or 2 and the cookies will loosen.) Roll each cookie around your finger or a wooden spoon handle to make curls. The cookies will harden in a few minutes. Keep them dry in a covered container.
Makes approximately 4 dozen

BUTTERSCOTCH OATMEAL COOKIES
(First Prize Winner at the "Little Farm Fair" in Berkeley)

Mix together well in a 3-quart bowl:
1-1/2 cups whole-wheat flour
1 teaspoon baking soda
1 teaspoon salt
1 cup oil
1/2 cup powdered milk
1 cup brown sugar
2 eggs
1 tablespoon hot water
1 cup butterscotch bits (if you get chunks, run through a meat grinder)
2 cups oatmeal
1 teaspoon vanilla extract
1/2 cup chopped walnuts
Place heaping spoonfuls far apart on a greased cookie sheet. Bake at 375° for 10 to 12 minutes. Let cool before removing from pan.
Makes approximately 4 dozen

SNICKERDOODLES

Mix together in a 3-quart bowl:
1 cup oil, or
1/4 pound butter, softened
1 cup brown sugar
2 eggs
1/2 teaspoon salt, or
1-1/2 teaspoons salt if using oil
1/2 cup powdered milk
2-3/4 cups flour
1 teaspoon baking soda
2 teaspoons cream of tartar
Roll small bits of the dough
into 3/4-inch balls.
Mix together:
4 tablespoons sugar
4 teaspoons cinnamon
Roll the balls in this mixture to
coat and place on a greased
cookie sheet. Flatten balls with
a fork twice at right angles and
bake at 400° for 8 to 10 minutes.
Makes 3 to 4 dozen

HONEY KISSES
(Teiglach)

Blend together:
3 eggs
2 tablespoons salad oil
Sift together:
2 cups unsifted flour
1 teaspoon baking powder
pinch salt
Then gradually add eggs and oil
to flour. Turn out on a lightly
floured board and knead until
smooth. Divide dough into 4
parts. Shape each part into a
1/2-inch-thick roll. Cut rolls
into 1/2-inch pieces.
Combine and heat to a boil
over medium heat:
2 cups honey
2/3 cup sugar
2 teaspoons powdered ginger
Drop pieces of dough into honey
mixture a few at a time so it
continues to boil.
When all pieces have been added,
cover and cook over low heat
for 20 minutes. Stir, then cook
for 5 minutes longer, or until
pieces are golden brown.
Remove to a wet surface to cool.
Store in a covered container.
Makes 4 to 5 dozen

MOLASSES CRACKERS

Stir together well:
2 tablespoons oil
2 tablespoons honey
2 tablespoons blackstrap
   molasses
1 tablespoon nutritional yeast
1 tablespoon soy flour
1 tablespoon wheat germ
1 teaspoon vanilla extract
1/4 teaspoon salt
1 egg
1 cup unsifted whole-wheat flour
Place dough on a well-floured
pastry cloth and roll out about
1/8 inch thick with a well-floured
rolling pin. You may want to add
additional flour to top of the
dough before you roll it out. Cut
the dough into squares and
place on ungreased cookie sheets.
Bake at 350° for 18 to 20
minutes.
Makes 2 dozen

SWEDISH SPICE COOKIES

Blend together in a bowl:
8-1/2 cups flour
1 teaspoon baking soda
1/2 teaspoon salt
Boil together in a saucepan
until sugar is dissolved:
1 cup sorghum or other thick
    syrup
1 cup sugar
Combine with syrup and gradually add to flour:
1 cup whipping cream
1 tablespoon cinnamon
1/4 pound butter
1 teaspoon powdered ginger
1/4 teaspoon ground cloves
dash nutmeg and cardamom
Let the dough sit in the refrigerator overnight or for several
days. Then roll it out and cut
out cookies. Bake at 375° until
light brown, about 10 minutes.
Makes 4 to 6 dozen

GINGERBREAD COOKIES

Mix together well:
1/2 cup each butter and oil, or
1 cup oil
1/3 cup powdered milk
2/3 cup brown sugar
1 egg
4 cups whole-wheat flour
1 teaspoon or more salt
1 teaspoon allspice
1 teaspoon cinnamon
1 teaspoon ground cloves
2 tablespoons powdered ginger
1/2 teaspoon baking soda
1 cup blackstrap molasses (it is
    best to measure the molasses
    in the cup you used to measure
    the oil)
2 tablespoons hot water
    (optional)
1/4 to 1/2 cup nutritional yeast
    (optional)
1 to 2 tablespoons dried kelp
    (optional)
Using a floured rolling pin, roll
out on a floured pastry board or
cloth to 1/4 inch thickness,
adding flour as needed. Cut into
shapes and bake at 350° for 10
to 15 minutes. It is not necessary
to grease the cookie sheets.

"PARENTS"

Mix together well:
1/2 pound butter, softened
1 cup vegetable oil
1-1/3 cups brown sugar
3 eggs, beaten until pale
2 teaspoons grated orange peel
2 tablespoons orange juice
3-1/4 cups sifted whole-wheat
    flour
1/2 teaspoon salt
2 teaspoons baking powder
Shape dough into a firm cylin-
drical roll about 2 inches in
diameter. Cover and chill at least
3 hours. Slice and bake on
greased cookie sheets in a 325°
oven for 12 to 15 minutes.
Makes approximately 3 dozen

STRUDEL DOUGH

Combine:
3 cups less 2 heaping tablespoons sifted flour
1/2 teaspoon salt
(Reserve the 2 tablespoons flour for use later.)
Beat:
1 egg, broken into
1/4 cup oil
Make a well in the flour, add oil-egg mixture and:
approximately 1 cup warm water
Beat until well blended. Turn out on board and knead gradually, working the 2 tablespoons reserved flour into the dough. Knead until dough is no longer sticky. Hit dough hard against the board about 150 times. Then cover surface of dough lightly with oil. Place in a covered bowl, let rest for 30 minutes and proceed to stretch the dough. (The dough must be warm.)

To Stretch the Dough:
Cover a table (about 48 x 30 inches) with a clean cloth and sprinkle cloth evenly with about:
1/2 cup low gluten or
pastry flour
Place dough on center of cloth and sprinkle very lightly with flour. Roll dough into a rectangle 1/4 to 1/8 inch thick. Clench fists, tucking the thumbs under the fingers. With the palm side of fists down, reach under the dough to its center (dough will rest on back of hands). Being careful not to tear dough, stretch the center gently and steadily toward you as you slowly walk around the table. (The dough should not have any torn spots, if possible, but such perfection will come only with practice.) As the center becomes as thin as paper, concentrate the stretching motion closer to the edge of the dough. Continue until dough is as thin as tissue paper, and hangs over edges of the table.
Trim the edges with scissors, leaving 2 inches of dough overhanging the table edge on all sides. Allow stretched dough to dry about 5 minutes until it is no longer sticky. Avoid drying it too long or it will become brittle. Brush oil or melted better over the dough, cover with filling and roll it up with a pushing action rather than the way you would roll a newspaper. (Spoon fillings on thinly so they don't run out when you bite into the strudel.) Place on a buttered baking sheet, flatten slightly and slit the strudel every 1-1/2 inches. Bake at 375° for 25 to 30 minutes, or until golden.

STRUDEL FILLINGS

- Apricot preserves, chopped walnuts and flaked coconut.
- Orange marmalade, chocolate bits and flaked almonds.
- Raspberry preserves, sesame seeds, chopped nuts and grated lemon rind.
- Chopped cooked apple, cinnamon and raisins.
- Pitted cooked cherries, almonds, coconut and cinnamon.
- Ground poppy seeds, chopped pecans and honey.
- Cottage cheese, sour cream and sautéed minced onion.
- The filling for spinach pie (page 28).

Beans

Bean buying is frustrating. The best prices of the year are in September when the crop comes in. If you can buy all the beans you will need for the year at one time, this is the month to do it. Since you probably can't do this, due to lack of funds and/or storage space, you must sit by and watch the price of beans rise through the next August. During the year the price on one or two types of beans may double. You can't even tell in advance which ones it will be; one year it was kidney beans, the year before it was pintos. You can, however, save money over the store price at any time of the year just by buying in bulk. Restaurant suppliers sell 10-, 25-, 50- and 100-pound sacks. So do institutional suppliers and bakery suppliers. If your order gets up to one or two thousand pounds you could ask local bean brokers if they will sell to you. (They are listed in the yellow pages under "beans"; you may need to get phone books for the big cities near you.) Special beans like mung, soy and azuki may have to be bought from suppliers of Oriental food.

Sometimes salvage houses get sacks of beans and split peas that have accidentally broken open. They will sell whatever remains in the sack at a lower price per pound than the intact sack would have cost. Some salvage houses are less honest than others. Some will sweep up spilled beans from the floor, dirt and all, and sell you the sack, including the dirt in the weight. Always rinse beans that you have bought from salvagers; we bought some salvaged oatmeal once and found little metal screws and hooks in it. Buying beans in bulk will save you about one-third over store prices or about one-half if you buy them from salvage houses.

Try to concentrate your orders on a few varieties of beans at first. While some members might prefer split peas over lentils, they would probably order lentils if split peas were not on the list. The added volume might make it possible for you to buy a 10-pound sack of lentils at wholesale. After your conspiracy grows, you will be able to offer both split peas and lentils. In Berkeley we once got to the point where we offered four types of rice. Do beans the same way you do grains.

Beans/How to Eat It

HOW TO SPROUT BEANS

Place in a 1-quart jar:

1/2 cup beans (mung, whole peas, pinto, etc.)

Pour over the beans and let soak overnight:

approximately 1-1/2 cups water

Place 2 4-inch-square pieces of cheesecloth over the jar opening and secure with a rubberband. Turn the jar upside down and drain off as much water as possible. Then place the jar upside down on a dish draining rack. Rinse the beans with water once or twice a day. Remove any that get moldy. Within a week, the sprouts should be ready to eat. (Note: For best results, use beans from the current year's crop.) If you want to avoid a "planty" taste in your sprouts, cover the jar with a towel to keep out light and thereby prevent the formation of chlorophyll.

HOW TO COOK BEANS

Soak overnight:

1 cup beans

3 cups water

In the morning, taste the water. If it is bitter, throw it out and replace with fresh water. Cook the beans in the water at a low boil, covered, until the skin of the bean breaks when you blow on it. Add extra water during cooking if necessary. (If you are in a real hurry, cook them in a pressure cooker, 45 minutes for most beans, 20 minutes for mung and azuki and 8 minutes for split peas and lentils.)

HUMOUS
(Middle Eastern Bean Paste)

Purée in blender or with a mortar and pestle:

3 cups cooked garbanzo beans

1/4 cup olive oil

Add to puréed beans:

paprika and chopped parsley to taste

juice of several lemons

4 tablespoons sesame tahini (page 115)

Serve as a dip or sandwich spread. Makes 6 sandwiches, or serves 16 as a dip

SOY SPREAD

Soak overnight:

1 cup soybeans

3 cups water

Discard soaking water and cook soybeans in an equal amount fresh water until the skins break when you blow on them. Then put the beans into a blender jar and add, blending until pasty:

3 tablespoons or more Tamari soy sauce

chili powder, garlic powder, dill weed and cayenne pepper to taste

2 carrots, chopped

2 celery stalks, chopped

1 to 2 onions, chopped and sautéed if desired

1/2 cup chopped parsley

anything else you'd like

Adjust consistency with water or more soy sauce if necessary.

Serves 6 to 8

MIDDLE EASTERN LENTIL SOUP

Place in a large pot:
1 pound washed lentils (green are the nicest)
2 onions, cut up
1 or 2 carrots, sliced
1 celery stalk, sliced
a large piece lamb breast, cut up
1 bay leaf, split in two
2 teaspoons salt
pepper
water to cover
(The lamb breast can be roasted for 30 minutes in a hot oven to get rid of excess fat, or put it in unroasted and worry about skimming off the fat later.) Bring to a boil and skim off fat. Cook over low heat for about 2 hours. Taste and adjust with salt.
Squeeze into pot:
juice of 2 to 3 garlic cloves
juice of 1/2 lemon
For a pretty green color, toss in just before serving:
chopped, cooked spinach (optional)
Serves 6

RED AND YELLOW BEAN SALAD

Drain well and place in a bowl:
2 cups cooked garbanzo beans
2 cups cooked kidney beans
Sauté until the onions are soft:
1 to 2 onions, chopped
1/4 to 1/2 pound mushrooms, chopped (optional)
oil
Add the sautéed vegetables to the beans.
To make dressing, mix together:
2 teaspoons salt
1/2 teaspoon cayenne pepper
3/4 teaspoon dry mustard
1/2 teaspoon paprika
1 garlic clove, chopped
2 tablespoons chopped chives
1/2 cup olive oil or safflower oil
2 tablespoons pickle relish
3 tablespoons vinegar
juice of 1 lemon
Add dressing to the beans, mixing thoroughly so all the beans are coated. Place in the refrigerator overnight, or for at least 2 hours, before serving. Keep covered or it will smell up your whole refrigerator.

DO-IT-YOURSELF TORTILLA SALAD

Heat in a little oil:
1/2 to 3/4 cup refried beans per person (page 109)
In separate pan, sauté in oil until translucent:
1 large onion, chopped
Add to sautéed onion:
1/2 to 3/4 cup chopped ripe olives
Set out buffet style:
the refried beans
the onion-olive mixture
1/2 to 1 pound grated cheese
corn chips or heated tortillas
tomato or hot sauce
chopped green pepper
sour cream
lettuce torn in pieces
Let the people help themselves. The corn, beans and cheese complement each other to make complete proteins.
Serves 4

INDIAN DAHL

Bring to a boil in a heavy pot
with a tight-fitting lid:
1 cup Indian lentils, split peas,
   mung beans or brown lentils
2 cups water
1 teaspoon salt
1/2 teaspoon turmeric
1/4 teaspoon ground red pepper
Simmer until beans are tender
and all the water is absorbed.
Fry together in a skillet:
1 onion, thinly sliced lengthwise
1 teaspoon cumin seeds
1/2 teaspoon ground coriander
3 tablespoons butter or
   crude safflower oil
When onions are golden, add
them to the cooked beans, stir,
cover the pot and let steam for a
few minutes. Serve with brown
rice or bulgur. A delicious,
sensual meal. Also cheap.
Serves 4

DAHL OF YELLOW SPLIT PEAS

Combine and boil gently without
covering until tender, adding
water as needed (or pressure cook
for 8 minutes):
3/4 cup yellow split peas
1 teaspoon salt
2 cups boiling water
Fry in pan until onions are
translucent:
2 cups minced onions
2 tablespoons butter or ghee
Make a massala by grinding
together:
1-1/2 teaspoons curry powder
pinch dry mustard
1/2 teaspoon turmeric
Add the spices to the onion and
cook slowly to a paste. Add paste
to peas and cook for about 15
minutes. Slow cooking is the
secret. Dahl should be thin
enough to run down into the
rice when it is spooned over it.
Serve topped with:
minced parsley, if desired
Serves 4

REFRIED BEANS

Soak overnight:
1 cup pinto beans
2-1/2 to 3 cups water
In a 2-quart pot place beans,
soaking water and:
1 tablespoon oil
Boil until beans are done and can
be easily mashed. Mash the beans
with a potato masher or a fork,
working into the beans at the
same time:
1/2 pound or more Monterey
   Jack cheese, grated
4 tablespoons hot taco sauce
1/2 cup chopped onions,
   sautéed if desired
Beans may be reheated in an
oiled skillet or in the oven
topped with:
more cheese
tomato slices for garnish

Beans/How to Eat It

SPICY GARBANZO BALLS
(Felafel)

Soak overnight:
1 cup garbanzo beans
3 cups water
Drain and run the beans through
a meat grinder on a medium
blade.
Mix ground garbanzos in a
bowl with:
1/4 cup bulgur wheat, soaked
    at least 1 hour in
3/4 cup water
1 egg
1/4 teaspoon cayenne pepper or
    chili pepper
3 tablespoons whole-wheat flour
2 to 3 garlic cloves, minced
1/4 teaspoon ground coriander
1 teaspoon salt
1 teaspoon cumin or
    curry powder
Form mixture into 3/4-inch
balls using a melon ball scooper
or small eating spoon.
Deep fry the balls until very
lightly browned in:
hot oil (350° to 375°)
Drain the balls on paper before
eating. These are often served
with humous.

Street vendors in Israel serve
these balls inside half a pita. A
dilute tahini sauce and a hot
sauce are poured over them. The
whole thing is topped with a
salad of mint leaves, cucumbers
and tomatoes with oil and
vinegar dressing.
Serves 4 to 6

DEEP-FRIED PEAS
OR SOYBEANS

Have ready:
dried whole peas or soybeans,
    soaked overnight, drained and
    patted dry
3 to 4 inches hot oil (350°)
Place a handful of peas or beans
at a time into a strainer. Lower
the strainer into the hot oil.
Cover the pan immediately to
keep from being burned if the
oil splatters. Keep the peas or
beans in the oil for at least
10 minutes, or until they are
crisp and not easily poked with
a fork.
Drain the peas or beans and add
before serving:
salt to taste
These go well with cooked
azuki beans or onions.

AZUKI-BEAN
MEAT SUBSTITUTE

Soak overnight:
1 cup azuki beans
3 cups water
Drain beans, saving soaking
water, and run beans through
a meat grinder. Return them
to their soaking water to cook,
covered, until done.
This doesn't taste like meat, even
if you add soy sauce, but it does
look like it on top of a pizza or
in lasagne. You can also make it
into patties with egg and herbs
and fry like hamburgers.
Serves 4

TUNISIAN LENTILS

Cook together in a covered pot
for about 30 minutes:
1 pound lentils
water to cover
1 bay leaf, split in two
1 or more garlic cloves
minced hot red pepper to taste
Add to lentils and cook
10 minutes:
salt to taste
1 teaspoon ground cumin
Serve over rice.
Serves 4

PEANUT-LENTIL STEW WITH POPPY-SEED SAUCE

Simmer together in a 3-quart pot until lentils are almost done:
1-1/2 cups washed lentils
1-1/2 quarts stock, or
2 tablespoons bouillon,
    dissolved in 1-1/2 quarts water
1/2 teaspoon salt
1 tablespoon celery seeds
3 tablespoons nutritional
    yeast (optional)
Add to pot and simmer until carrots are warm and slightly soft:
3 celery stalks, coarsely chopped
2 yellow onions, coarsely chopped
3 carrots, sliced in thick rounds
4 cups cut-up tomatoes
2 tablespoons oil
1 tablespoon lemon juice
1 to 2 tablespoons curry powder
Add and continue simmering until peanuts are warm through:
shelled peanuts from 1 pound
    roasted peanuts

To Make Poppy Seed Sauce:
Combine and heat:
1/2 pound poppy seeds, freshly
    ground
water, as needed for desired
    consistency
(The poppy seeds can be ground in a hand mill, a blender or a mortar and pestle.) Spoon sauce over stew. This sauce can also be made with sesame seeds (toasted or raw), salt and garlic and maybe some lemon juice.
Serves 8 to 10

CHILI

Soak overnight and drain:
2 pounds kidney beans
water as needed for soaking
Brown:
2 large onions, chopped
2 pounds ground beef
In a large pot, place:
the drained kidney beans
the browned onions and beef
3 pounds tomatoes, chopped
2 tablespoons chili powder
salt and cayenne pepper to taste
Simmer chili until done, about 2 to 3 hours.
Makes 6 quarts

LOUISE'S BAKED BEANS

Soak overnight:
4 cups navy beans
water as needed for soaking
Cook beans in soaking water until skins break when you blow on them. Drain the beans and reserve the cooking liquid.
Place in a large bean pot:
the drained navy beans
1/4 cup oil
2 teaspoons or more salt
3 tablespoons brown sugar
1/2 cup blackstrap molasses
rounded 1/2 teaspoon dry
    mustard
1 very large onion, chopped
1 cup dry white wine
1 ham bone (optional)
1 to 2 bay leaves
Add the reserved liquid to the pot, adding water if necessary to cover. Cover the pot and bake at 250° for 8 hours without stirring. Add water as needed to keep beans covered. Uncover pot last 30 minutes to let beans dry out.
Serves 16

111

Nuts, Seeds and Dried Fruit

When buying nuts, seeds and dried fruit, ask for a taste first! Quality varies from crop to crop and from supplier to supplier. Price is no indication of quality. The best sources for these items are bakery supply houses, which often carry several levels of quality for different purposes. The owners of these warehouses are also frequently willing to bargain, particularly on "low quality" foods.

QUALITY   The quality you want and the quality that bakery suppliers charge for are two different things. You want flavor; they charge extra for appearance, because bakeries want the perfect nuts for decorating their products. "Sheller run" nuts (those that have been nicked in the shelling machine) sell for about 30 cents less per pound than those that weren't nicked. Broken sunflower seeds and pieces of walnuts, cashews and pecans sell for less than intact nuts and seeds. Dried apricots which are a pleasing shade of orange will sell for more money than brownish or torn ones. The main disadvantage of buying the cheapest foods available is that they might not taste as good as the quality that sells for more or they may be mixed with pieces of corn or even pebbles. These same problems may also be found in the higher-priced categories, however.

BUYING   Most bakery supply shops will sell nuts and seeds in any quantity over five pounds. A price break won't come until you buy a complete unit, like a 30-pound box or a 50-pound bag. You can, however, bargain. For example you can say to "Max," "How much is your tapioca? Hirsch Bros. is getting 39 cents." He will probably answer in one of three ways: "I can match that," or "You can have it for 35 cents," or "He's still got some of last year's crop; go buy it while it lasts. Mine just cost me 45 cents." If, on the other hand, "Max" is nasty and doesn't want to bargain, he will either respond: "Our price is 50 cents," or "If you want to know about prices, buy your stuff elsewhere." If "Max" is willing to bargain, be appreciative. Let him know that you like the price breaks and will give him as much as possible of your business.

Buying dried fruits is slightly different from buying nuts and seeds. Very few suppliers want to be bothered with weighing out quantities. (After all, the fruits are sticky.) Dried fruits usually come in 30-pound boxes; some items like apricots may come in five-pound bags, bleached raisins in 10-pound boxes and pitted dates in 17-1/2-pound boxes. If you explain to "Max" that you have advance money for only 14 pounds of dates, he may cut the price so you can buy the 17-1/2 pounds for only 50 cents over the amount you planned to spend.

If there are no bakery suppliers in your area, you should look for dried fruit at the farmer's market and ask restaurant suppliers for nuts and seeds. Restaurant suppliers usually won't bargain. They also tend to have everything prepackaged in 1-, 5- and 25-pound units. Sellers at the farmers' market are usually very willing to bargain when customers offer to take large quantities like 20 or 30 pounds.

Dried fruits, seeds and nuts should be bagged the same way as grains. You must, however, take a slightly higher markup on them and buy a little more than is ordered to account for the inevitable nibbling. For example, a 30-pound box of raisins usually yields 29-1/2 pounds after bagging.

Other sources for nuts and fruit include pick-it-yourself orchards. Watch the "market basket" section of the want ads in your local newspaper. This is a good way to get nuts if you don't mind hulling and shelling them. You could even try drying your own fruits. It can be done in a kiln or a low-temperature oven (200° or below) or in the sun, covered with cheesecloth to keep off bugs.

Any supplier you can find for nuts, seeds and dried fruit will save you money compared with the grocery-store price as they are high markup items. Because they are expensive they are "slow movers" and cost a store more to handle than "fast movers." Thus the stores raise the markup on these items to cover their costs, making them even more expensive.

TOASTED SESAME SEEDS

Have ready:
1/2 cup or more raw sesame seeds
1 cast-iron pan in need of
    seasoning
Place the seeds in the pan over
medium heat and push them
around with a wooden spoon
until they brown and smell good;
some of the seeds will make pop-
ping noises. The pan will be
seasoned by the sesame oil that
escapes from the seeds while
they are toasting.

TAHINI

Pulverize in a blender:
1 cup toasted sesame seeds
1 teaspoon salt
Add to blender and grind to
smooth paste:
2 garlic cloves, chopped
pinch cayenne pepper
juice of 1 lemon
1/2 cup or more water
The consistency of the paste will
depend on how the tahini is to
be used. It should be thick for a
dip, thinner for a sauce.
Makes approximately 1-1/2 cups

SOY WALNUTS

Place in a heavy pan over
low heat:
1/2 cup walnuts
1 teaspoon soy sauce
1 teaspoon butter
Push the walnuts around the pan
with a wooden spoon for 3 to 4
minutes, or until the nuts are
toasted. These are a good snack
or can be served as a side dish
with rice and pineapple.
Serves 4 as a side dish

HOW TO SPROUT
ALFALFA SEEDS

Place in the bottom of a 1-quart
canning jar:
1/4 cup alfalfa seeds
Cover the seeds with several
inches of water and let soak
overnight. The next day, cover
the mouth of the jar with 2 4-
inch-square layers of cheesecloth
and secure with a rubberband.
Pour off the soaking water
and place the jar upside down
in a dish draining rack.
Rinse the seeds with fresh water
once or twice a day until the
sprouts are crowding their way
out of the jar. This takes less
than 1 week.
Makes 1 quart

GRANOLA

Heat in a 350° oven for 10 minutes and then place in a 3-quart
bowl:
5 cups rolled oats
Add to bowl with oats and mix
together well:
scant 1/2 cup (not packed)
    brown sugar
1 cup wheat germ
3/4 cup flaked coconut
1 cup chopped walnuts
Stir into oats, coating well:
1/3 cup oil
Stir into oats, combining
thoroughly:
1/3 cup each molasses and honey
1 teaspoon vanilla
salt to taste
Spread this on 2 or 3 cookie
sheets and place in a 350° oven
for 20 minutes. Allow the granola
to cool and put in a large storage
container. Stir until crumbly.
Also makes a good ice cream
topping.
Serves 4 to 6

Nuts, Seeds and Dried Fruit/How to Eat It

DRIED FRUIT CHUTNEY

Place in a large kettle and let stand 24 hours:

4 apples, peeled, cored and run through a meat grinder or chopped
1 quart cider vinegar
2 cups unfiltered apple juice
1 cup pitted dates, ground in meat grinder
3/4 cup currants, chopped

Add to fruit mixture and simmer for 45 to 60 minutes, stirring occasionally until mixture is thick:

2 cups brown sugar or honey
3 tablespoons salt
2 tablespoons chopped candied ginger
1/2 teaspoon cayenne pepper

Pour into sterilized jars and seal. Or, pressure can for 10 minutes at 10 pounds pressure.
Makes approximately 3 quarts

BANANA AND DATE CHUTNEY

Cook together in a heavy pot until dates, onions and bananas are tender:

12 slightly green bananas, peeled and sliced
6 medium-sized yellow onions, peeled and chopped
1 pound dried dates, chopped
2-1/2 cups distilled or cider vinegar

Put in a blender or mixing bowl and blend or beat until the mixture is a pulp. Add to fruit and cook until chutney is a deep brown:

2 teaspoons curry powder, or
1 teaspoon each allspice and coriander and a pinch turmeric
1/2 pound sugared ginger, run through a meat grinder
1 tablespoon salt
1-1/3 cups dark molasses

These ingredients are available year round, so this chutney can be made any time. Serve immediately, or can at 10 pounds pressure for 10 minutes.
Makes approximately 3 quarts

APRICOT MINCEMEAT

Run through a meat grinder on a coarse blade, including the sugar if it needs it:

1 pound dried apricots, soaked overnight in a little water
1 pound pitted dates
1 pound currants
2 cups suet (butter may be substituted and added after grinding)
1 pound apples, peeled, cored and chopped
1 pound seed-free raisins
2 cups or less brown sugar
1/4 cup or more almonds

Add to above:

minced rind and juice of 1 lemon
1 to 3 tablespoons grated nutmeg

Use immediately, or can at 10 pounds pressure for 10 minutes.
Makes approximately 3 quarts

APRICOT NUT BREAD

Mix together:
2 cups whole-wheat flour
1/2 teaspoon salt
1 teaspoon baking soda
1 teaspoon baking powder
1 egg
1 tablespoon butter or oil
2/3 cup brown sugar
1/3 cup powdered milk
1 cup orange juice or water
1 cup dried apricots, run through
   a meat grinder
1/2 cup chopped walnuts,
   pecans or almonds
Pour into a greased loaf pan and
bake at 350° for 50 to 60
minutes.
Makes 1 loaf

DATE CAKE

Have ready:
1 cup pitted and chopped dates
1 teaspoon baking soda
1-1/2 cups boiling water
Place dates and soda into a bowl
and pour boiling water over
them.

Mix together:
1/4 pound butter, softened
1/4 cup sugar
2 eggs, beaten
Combine dates and sugar-butter
mixture. Sift together and add
to date mixture:
1-1/2 cups whole-wheat flour
1/3 teaspoon salt
3/4 teaspoon baking soda
Pour batter into an oblong cake
pan and sprinkle top with:
1 cup chocolate bits
1/2 cup chopped pecans
1/2 cup brown sugar
Bake at 350°for 35 to 40 minutes.

RAW CANDY OR FRUIT NUT BALLS

Mix together:
3/4 cup Brazil nuts, chopped
3/4 cup broken pecans
1 cup raisins
1 cup dates, pitted and
   finely chopped
2 tablespoons honey
2 tablespoons minced lemon
   or orange rind, or
1 to 2 tablespoons mace
Form the mixture into balls and
roll, until coated, in:
1-1/2 cups flaked coconut
Sunflower seeds may be substituted for some of the nuts.
Makes approximately 3 dozen

ELIZABETH'S WHOLE-WHEAT SESAME CRACKERS

Mix together thoroughly:
3/4 cup sesame seeds
1/4 pound butter, softened
Cut into butter:
2 scant cups whole-wheat flour
Sprinkle onto dough and work
into a ball, handling as little
as possible:
2 tablespoons water
Roll out very thin on a floured
board and cut into diamonds or
squares. Prick each cracker twice
with a fork. Place crackers on an
ungreased baking sheet and bake
at 400° for 10 minutes, or until
bottom changes color slightly.
Remove to rack and let cool
thoroughly. Delicious!
Makes 3 dozen 2-inch crackers

APRICOT, PECAN, COCONUT DROP COOKIES

Mix together:
2 cups pecans, chopped
1 cup dried apricots, run
   through a meat grinder on
   medium blade
2 eggs, beaten
1 cup honey
Let stand at room temperature
for 1 hour, or overnight in a
refrigerator, so dried apricots
can soak up as much honey as
possible.
Stir into above mixture to soak
up remaining honey:
1 cup or more unsweetened
   flaked coconut
Drop by spoonfuls onto buttered
brown paper on a cookie sheet.
Bake at 375° for about 10 minutes or until lightly browned.
Makes 4 to 5 dozen

FILBERT COOKIES

Mix together well:
1-1/2 cups whole-wheat flour
1/4 teaspoon cinnamon
1/4 teaspoon cocoa or carob
   powder
3/4 cup softened sweet butter
1/2 teaspoon lemon juice
3/4 cup powdered or
   brown sugar
2 tablespoons water, if needed
   to handle dough
Mix in:
1/2 cup ground filberts
Form batter into a log 1-1/2
inches in diameter and slice off
1/4-inch or thinner rounds. Bake
the rounds at 325° for about
12 minutes.
Spread half of the cookies with:
raspberry jam
Spread the remaining half with:
partially melted chocolate bits
Place the chocolate-topped
cookies on the jam ones. Place
on top of each:
1 almond
If you put the almond in place
before the chocolate hardens,
it will stick nicely.
Makes 3 dozen

PECAN COOKIES
(With Chocolate Frosting)

Mix together, adding one
ingredient at a time to make
mixing thorough and easy:
2-1/2 cups flour
1 pound butter, softened
1 egg
1-1/3 cups powdered sugar
1 teaspoon vanilla extract
2 cups ground pecans
Roll dough in small balls and
place on cookie sheet. Bake
at 375° for 10 minutes.

To Make Frosting:
Melt in double boiler:
1 cup chocolate bits
Beat together and add to
chocolate:
1 egg
1/4 pound butter, softened
Mix until well blended. Ice the
cookies. These are easy to make
and delicious.
Makes 4 to 5 dozen

CRISS' CRAZY MACAROONS

Mix together:
2 whole eggs, or
4 egg whites
1-1/2 teaspoons vanilla extract
1/2 teaspoon almond extract
1 teaspoon salt
2-1/2 cups grated coconut
1/2 cup sesame seeds
1 cup pumpkin or sunflower
    seeds, chopped
2 cups brown sugar
Drop by spoonfuls onto buttered
brown paper on a cookie sheet
and bake at 325° for about
20 minutes.
Makes 2 dozen

HAMANTASCHEN

To Make Pastry:
Mix together well:
4 cups whole-wheat flour
2 teaspoons baking powder
1/2 cup brown sugar
pinch salt
4 eggs, well beaten
1/3 cup oil
Roll out thinly on a floured cloth
or board. Cut into rounds with
the lid off a 1-pound peanut
butter jar.

To Make Filling:
Mix together:
1 pound poppy seeds, ground
4 tablespoons honey
Cook over low heat in a heavy
pan for 5 minutes or until the
mixture is warmed through.
Add to above mixture and mix
in well:
1 egg
juice of 1/2 lemon
1/2 cup chopped walnuts
    or pecans
Place a spoonful of filling onto
each pastry round and trap it
there by bringing up the sides of
the round to form a 3-sided pyra-
mid. Pinch the edges together.
Brush the hamantaschen with:
1 egg white, beaten (optional)
Bake the cookies at 375° for
20 minutes. These cookies keep
well for weeks.
Makes about 5 dozen

CANDIED PEEL

Have ready:
8 oranges or lemons, or
4 each oranges and lemons
Wash fruit and cut oranges in
half crosswise and lemons in half
vertically. Remove all pulp.
Dissolve and pour over peels:

1/2 teaspoon baking soda, in
1/4 cup hot water
Pour over peels to cover:
boiling water
Let stand 20 minutes and then
rinse peels several times. Place
peels in saucepan and cover with:
cold water
Bring to a boil and continue
boiling until peels are tender.
Combine to make a syrup:
1 pound white sugar
2 scant cups water
Pour syrup over peels and let
stand for 2 days. Draw off syrup.
Add to syrup:
1 cup white sugar
Put peels back into syrup and
bring to a boil. Boil until peels
look clear. Take the peels out of
the syrup and dry them in a 200°
or lower oven. Meanwhile, reduce
the syrup by boiling it for 30
minutes. Dip the peels into the
syrup and dry them again in a
200° oven. If a sweeter peel is
desired, beat the remaining
syrup until cloudy, pour it into
the cup side of the peels and
dry them again.

Herbs and Spices

Herbs and spices are expensive. By buying them from restaurant and institutional suppliers, you can get a better quality for half the price you would pay in a store. You will, however, have to purchase them in one-pound containers. That can be insignificant in the case of items like mustard which runs 60 to 90 cents per pound or horrendous with spices like cardamom which runs $8 to $16 per pound. We usually ask each member to order in four-ounce units. That amount is easy to weigh and fits into an empty jam jar. The general rule is that we will buy a one-pound container of a cheap spice if one-half pound is ordered; we will buy a pound of a medium-price spice if 3/4 pound is ordered and we will buy a pound of an expensive spice only when a whole pound is ordered. It is essential to have an accurate scale when weighing spices. You can go broke quickly if you aren't careful. Use a postage scale or a double-beam balance baby scale (without springs). Be sure members specify whole or ground spices and herbs when ordering.

If your orders get to be one-pound multiples you could check into buying from distributors (listed under "spices" in the yellow pages) and possibly mail ordering herbs from places like Lhasa Karnak Herb Company, 2482 Telegraph Avenue, Berkeley, California; Nature's Herb Company, 281 Ellis Street, San Francisco; or Green Mountain Herbs, Ltd., 720 Pearl Street, Boulder, Colorado. Be sure to tell these companies that you are a business and thereby get their business discount.

Any extras should be stored in glass jars and offered as impulse buys at distribution time. If any are left over after that, store them in a dark place and offer them for sale at your next distribution.

Herbs and spices are very easy to do. Most restaurant suppliers will deliver. Usually, you will only have to fill four bags from each container. If five people order the same spice, you could give four people three ounces and one person four ounces.

ALL-OF-A-SUDDEN PESTO
(Basil Sauce)

Melt in a small frying pan:
1/4 pound butter, or
1/2 cup olive oil, or
1/4 cup each butter and olive oil
Mix into butter and/or oil and
simmer until parsley is well
cooked:
2 tablespoons or more dried basil
10 or more parsley sprigs,
    finely chopped
8 garlic cloves, minced
salt to taste
Mix sauce into:
1/2 pound noodles, cooked
(Spinach noodles are very good
with this sauce.) Then mix in:
1/2 to 1 cup grated Parmesan
    cheese
Serves 2 to 4

NASTURTIUM SAUCE

Simmer for 10 minutes:
5 cups vinegar
1 small onion, chopped
6 whole cloves
1 teaspoon salt
1/2 teaspoon cayenne pepper
Add to mixture:
5 cups pressed nasturtium
    flowers
Cover for 2 months. Strain
and add:
1 teaspoon soy sauce
Pour into a sterile bottle and
cork tightly. Use as a sauce over
vegetables and rice.
Makes approximately 5 cups

CREAMY ITALIAN
DRESSING

Mix together and store in
a glass bottle or jar:
3/4 cup mayonnaise
1 tablespoon wine vinegar
1 tablespoon lemon juice
1 tablespoon oil
1 tablespoon water
1 teaspoon Worcestershire sauce
1/2 teaspoon dried oregano leaves
1 small garlic clove, minced
drop of honey (optional)
Makes approximately 1 cup

SHARYN AND DAVE'S
HOT SAUCE

Put in a blender and liquefy:
1 pound tomatoes, cored
    and cut up
2 or 3 hot red chili peppers,
    finely chopped
6 or more garlic cloves, minced
1/2 teaspoon salt
2 tablespoons red wine vinegar
1 to 2 teaspoons dried basil
    (optional)
1 green onion, finely chopped, or
1/4 yellow onion, finely chopped
Heat in a small pan over low heat
for 3 to 4 minutes. Do not boil.
This sauce is hot, but not so hot
that it is hard to use.
Makes approximately 3 cups

ZAPPO FOR VEGETABLES

Stir together:
1 cup olive oil
2 tablespoons wine vinegar
salt, pepper, basil and
    oregano to taste
a bit of sugar or honey
Refrigerate and use as
a marinade for sliced carrots,
celery, radishes, etc.
Makes about 1 cup

VINAIGRETTE

Combine and let stand for at
least 1 hour:
2 teaspoons salt
1/2 teaspoon freshly ground
    black pepper
3/4 teaspoon dry mustard
1/2 teaspoon paprika
1/4 teaspoon garlic powder
1 tablespoon finely chopped
    chives
1/2 cup olive oil
Add to oil mixture and beat
thoroughly:
2 tablespoons pickle relish
1 tablespoon finely chopped
    green pepper
3 tablespoons cider or wine
    vinegar
2 tablespoons freshly-squeezed
    lemon juice
Add to vegetables that have been
steamed until tender. A few
cloves of allspice in the steaming
water is nice. Cover and marinate
in the refrigerator about 1 hour,
or until the vegetables are cool.

MINTED MEATBALLS

Mix together, form into
meatballs and set aside:
1 pound ground beef
3 tablespoons chopped
    yellow onion
1 cup chopped tomatoes
1 garlic clove, chopped
1-1/2 tablespoons chopped
    fresh mint
1 egg
1/4 cup raw rice
salt and pepper to taste
Fry together in a soup pot or
baking dish:
1 onion, chopped (or more)
2 tomatoes, chopped (or more)
If you have fried the vegetables
in a soup pot add:
4 to 5 cups water
If you have fried the vegetables
in a baking dish add:
1/2 cup of water
Bring water in the soup pot
to boil, and drop in the meatballs.
Just put the meatballs into the
baking dish and place in a 350°
oven.
Boil or bake until done. The
soup pot method requires less
cooking time.
Serves 4

VEGETABLE LOAF

Mix together:
1/2 cup chopped raw potato
1/2 cup chopped carrots
1/2 cup chopped walnuts
1 medium-sized onion, sliced
Add to vegetables:
oregano, rosemary, thyme,
    parsley and minced garlic
    to taste
1/2 cup bread crumbs, mixed
    with some wheat germ
1 egg, beaten
1/2 cup tomato sauce
Place in a greased loaf pan and
bake at 350° for 45 minutes to
1 hour. When the loaf is almost
done, pour extra tomato sauce
on top to make it more colorful,
if you want.

MARIGOLDED APPLES
(With Other Herbs)

Place in a baking dish:
3 tart cooking apples, peeled, cored and cut into rings
Beat together:
2 eggs, beaten
1 cup milk
Add to milk and eggs and pour over apples:
1 teaspoon chopped marigold petals
1 teaspoon chopped fresh sweet thyme
1 teaspoon chopped fresh sage
pinch cayenne
Put on top:
2 pats butter (optional)
Bake at 325° for 25 minutes.
Serves 4 to 6

AFRICAN SPICE BREAD

Soak until foamy, about 10 minutes:
1 tablespoon yeast, in
1/4 cup warm water
Combine in a bowl:
2 eggs
1 cup honey
1 tablespoon ground coriander
1 teaspoon cinnamon
1/4 teaspoon ground cloves
1-1/2 teaspoons salt
1 cup warm water
4 tablespoons sweet butter, melted
Add yeast to the mixture and gradually stir in, using only enough to form a soft ball of dough:
approximately 4-1/2 cups unbleached white flour
Knead dough until smooth and elastic, adding while kneading:
2 tablespoons sweet butter, melted
Let dough rise for 1 hour in a greased bowl. Then knead the dough to get any large bubbles out. Shape the dough into a round and let rise in a greased bowl until almost double in bulk. Bake at 300° 1 hour. This bread is light and spicy, almost like a coffee cake. It is nice as dessert or as a pleasant change from ordinary bread.
Makes 1 loaf

SPICE CAKE

Mix together well:
2-1/2 cups whole-wheat flour
1 teaspoon baking powder
1 teaspoon baking soda
3/4 teaspoon salt
3/4 teaspoon cinnamon
1/2 teaspoon ground cloves
1-1/3 cups brown sugar
2/3 cup powdered milk
2/3 cup softened butter or oil
1 cup milk soured with lemon juice (if using oil, add 2 additional tablespoons sour milk)
2 eggs
generous 1/2 cup chopped walnuts (optional)
Pour in 2 well-greased, 8- or 9-inch cake pans with paper lining the bottoms. (To get the paper to fit, trace the outside of the pan on a sheet of typing paper or brown paper bag.) Bake approximately 25 minutes at 350°. Ice with super icing (page 97). You might want to put some instant coffee and lemon juice into the icing.

MINT JELLY

Have ready:
**1 cup firmly packed fresh
   mint leaves**
1 cup boiling water
Place mint leaves in a bowl and
pour the water over them. Let
stand for 1 hour. Pour into
a 3-quart pot:
**1 or 2 quarts unfiltered apple
   juice (tart is best)**
Add 2 tablespoons of the mint
extract per cup of apple juice
to the pot. Bring the juice to
a boil (216° to 220°) and check
to see if the liquid is thick and
will sheet off a spoon. If the
liquid is not thick, cook a while
longer. If it still doesn't thicken,
add some commercial pectin
following the instructions on
the package.
Pour the jelly into sterile jars
(adding some green food coloring if you want) and cap with
melted paraffin or a 2-part canning
lid. Use 1/2-pint canning jars, if
possible.
Makes 2 quarts

GARDEN TEA

Just about anything growing
around the house can be thrown
into your teapot with tasty
results. Some favorites are
parsley, raspberry leaves and
mint leaves.
Have ready:
**1 to 2 tablespoons (or more if
   you like strong tea) of
   desired leaves**
4 cups boiling water
Rinse a teapot with hot water.
Place leaves in the teapot or
a tea ball. Pour on the water
when boiling has stopped, cover
the pot and let steep for at least
5 minutes before drinking.
Serves 4

WHAT TO DO WITH
LEFTOVER HERBAL TEA

Most teas can be reheated by
pouring more boiling water into
the teapot with the remaining
tea and leaves. If you don't
want to do that, you can water
your plants with it; it perks
them up. Feed your plants the
tea leaves, too.

CINNAMON TEA

Boil together for 5 minutes:
3 cinnamon sticks
4 cups water
Add to taste:
lemon juice
honey or sugar
Serves 4

HOT SPICED APPLE JUICE

Heat in a glass pot or
enameled pan:
6 to 8 cups apple juice
**1/4 cup orange, lemon or lime
   slices with peel, or any com-
   bination of the 3**
1 2-inch stick cinnamon
4 to 6 cloves
Serve with orange, lemon or lime
slice in each mug.
You can also use coriander, nutmeg or other spices; or you can
use ground spices—it will look
funny, but taste good.
Serves 6 or 8

Conspiring to Buy
Non-Food Items

Caselot is canned food. It is also anything else that comes in a case like peanut butter, cast-iron pans, film, shampoo, toilet paper, canisters, noodles, pet food and clothing.

To get started, look in the yellow pages of your phone book under "grocers wholesale." Call those that interest you and ask for catalogues and price books (sometimes they are separate and you correlate the item to its price by its identifying code number). Pick one supplier to start with; you can get specialty items from the others after you have learned how to do caselots efficiently.

Go through the catalogue and pick out about 100 items you think members will want to order; list them giving their code number, can size, case quantity, case price and individual can price. (Be sure you get the code number right. You might get snail killer when you wanted sisal rope.) This list will give members an idea of what is available and they can look through the catalogue if they would like to order additional items. You can also stockpile toilet paper, light bulbs and other non-perishables when stores have them on special and sell them to members a package at a time as needed. This way you can get the best of both worlds; you can have "sale prices" on the "popular" items and wholesale prices on everything else you want.

Distribution of caselot is very much like that for grains, except that there is no bagging. You just deal out the items as they are listed on the item cards and members pick up their orders. If you have several conspiracies buying together you can divide by conspiracy at a central location and later give out the cases by member.

In most states non-food items are subject to sales tax which your conspiracy will have to collect from its members and pay to the state. This requires more complicated bookkeeping than with food items.

Conspiring to Buy Non-Food Items

OTHER MERCHANDISE   There are many items other than caselot on which your conspiracy can obtain wholesale prices. A local Levi's merchant sells us "seconds" at a discount, and we get work clothes from Key Industries of Fort Scott, Kansas. A local hardware-variety store gives us a discount on any merchandise from its catalogue that it does not regularly stock. The four-gallon and five-quart plastic canisters we use to store our grains come from a local pickle packer for 80 cents and 30 cents respectively. Kitchen Aid (Hobart) gives us one-third off on their appliances. Auto supply stores sell to us at the same prices that they give garage mechanics. While picking up the ink and paper for printing our lists at the stationery wholesaler, we also get cases of typewriter ribbon and reams of paper for members who want them.

Very few merchants have refused to sell to us; some however, have had minimum orders larger than we could handle. The only dodge we have found for that barrier has been to select some cheap things we could afford to stockpile and to order items that we knew the supplier had out of stock to build up our order to the minimum. In general we average 20 to 40 percent below store prices.

Another source you might consider is government surplus sales. The government ditches all sorts of good things like typewriters, trucks, donkeys, car parts, photo equipment, textiles, hay, etc.—all for whatever they can get. You can bid, too. Most items go for less than half what they cost on the regular market. You can get on the mailing list that gives notice of these sales by writing the General Services Administration, Denver, Colorado 80225. These sales, which are held all over the country, are where most of the government surplus stores get their merchandise.

Beware of broken items, of which there are many. Don't buy something that doesn't work unless you know how to fix it or are sure you know exactly what is wrong and how much the repair will cost. For $50 we bought an electric typewriter that was listed as having a broken carriage. It turned out to need over $300 in repairs. Fortunately, the government had misdescribed the typestyle, so they had to take it back and return our money. GSA claims to guarantee descriptions. But that is all they guarantee; they do not guarantee the merchandise, unless the description says "operable."

BOOKS   For orders up to five copies of any book, go to your local jobber (listed under "books wholesale" in the yellow pages). For more copies, go direct to the publisher. Most paperback books sell for 30 percent off at jobbers and 40 percent off plus shipping from the publisher. Estimate 10 cents shipping per book and send a check with your order. You should get your books within a month. For hardbacks, you can get a 40 percent discount on the single-copy order plan from most publishers.

Licenses / Keeping Records

Licenses are a nuisance! They are, however, easier to get while you are small and cute looking. The longer you wait, the more money and hassle they will cost. This doesn't mean you should rush right out and buy every license available. It does, however, mean that you should not procrastinate if a supplier says you need a certain license in order to buy from him, or if you find that you want a health inspector to check your premises or tell you some rules. If you approach the authorities to ask them for help or instruction, they will be a lot nicer than if they find out about you from a jealous local store owner who wants to shut you down. It is important to call yourself a food buying club when getting licenses and permits; the name has a good image.

If some members receive food stamps your conspiracy will want to be authorized to accept them. This permit is free. In order to get it you must write some by-laws in which there is a clause that says your group welcomes food-stamp customers. You will also have to draw up a change-credit coupon, worth 49 cents or less, that you will give to a food stamp customer who presents stamps worth more than the amount of food he is taking.

In order for the authorization to become final, you will have to set up a checking account in which you can deposit the stamps. (Nobody ever gives anybody cash for stamps. You give stamp customers food and change coupons for their stamps; the bank credits your account for the stamps you deposit; the Federal Reserve credits your bank's account; etc.) Many banks will open free accounts to nonprofit organizations. Since your conspiracy is one, ask around.

After you have your by-laws, change-credit coupons and bank account, send some members of your conspiracy who have good personal credit (i.e., don't bounce many checks) with copies of the by-laws and change-credit coupon to the nearest

Food Stamp Credit

¢ ≤ 49¢

Corner Street
Buying Club

Food and Nutrition Service Office of the Department of Agriculture. There, you will be asked to fill out forms and answer some questions, including the following:

• **Estimate your volume for the coming year.** Tell them that you are just getting started and really don't know. They will insist on an answer in order to fill out a blank on their form. Make a stink so the officials will remember that you didn't want to give them an amount, because if at the end of the year you weren't accurate, they will suspect you of dishonesty. The Albany Conspiracy estimated $30,000 volume and only did $27,000; this rated them two nasty phone calls. The People's Garden did a volume over their estimate and had their permit revoked.

• **We would like a complete list of your membership.** This request is not on their form and they are not entitled to the information. Since most of us felt that we had little enough privacy already, we told them that our members don't like to have their names on lists. It is, although the Office won't believe it, actually impossible for a food conspiracy to know at any given time who is and is not a member, once the group has grown to over 10 families. The Office is entitled only to the names, addresses and phone numbers of two members so they can be reached if some food stamps are stolen or some rules are changed. The Office also will send these people warnings in the guise of news bulletins: i.e., "Joe's Corner Market is having its authorization suspended for six months. A checker there was caught selling a tube of toothpaste for food stamps. By doing this Joe's Corner Market was not helping a needy family get more for its food dollar. This suspension does not preclude other legal or punitive action against Joe's Corner Market." Stores and groups get these notices all the time. Rarely will you have heard of the store that is being punished.

• **When can we watch your group in operation?** Most conspiracies distribute food on weekends and in the evenings. (Members have jobs, too.) The Food and Nutrition Service Office people only work during business hours. When you tell them how a conspiracy operates they will think that you are trying to thwart them. You could offer to put on a show for them during business hours once; after all, you are doing it right.

One drawback to the food-stamp program is that members must first pay money for their food, and then, when the food arrives, they get back their money and pay their stamps. It is illegal to take stamps from a member without immediately giving him his food. Write your congressman! Tell him that the law is discriminating against buying clubs.

RESALE PERMIT   If your state has a sales tax, you will need a permit in order to buy taxable items without paying the tax, and in order to collect the tax when your members

pay for these items. You will be required to pay this collected tax to the state approximately every three months—in some states it is every month. While you are small, wholesalers might be willing to collect your taxes for you. But after you get so big that they don't want to handle your taxes, you will be so big that the state will require a large deposit to insure that you will pay your taxes. Some businesses may not sell to you at all if you don't have this permit. Find out. Call your prospective suppliers and ask if you will need any permits to buy from them.

This particular permit is especially nuisancish because you are expected to keep records to justify the taxes you collect and pay. If a conspiracy in your area already has one, buy with them and offer to help with their bookkeeping. That conspiracy can become a miniature wholesaler for your area. To get a resale permit, send a businesslike member to the Board of Equalization, Tax Board or whatever the appropriate agency is called in your state. Have him explain what you are doing and stress how small you are. You may even get your deposit waived. If you have trouble, go to your legislature for help. You are entitled to a permit. Don't forget; you are buying things as a business and reselling them to members. Don't give the impression that you yourself are doing all the buying and eating.

BUSINESS LICENSE

The agency that issues your resale permit will probably notify your city that you exist. Some cities will ignore this because you are so small. Others will ask you to buy a business license. (When you file your taxes, your city will be sent a copy of the form you send in. City hall will therefore know when you get big enough for them to bother with.) This license will cost $20 to $30. This is another reason to let one conspiracy wholesale for the others. You can all help pay for the license. Try to get licensed as a home industry. Cities that have that category of license usually charge as little as $6.

If your state does not have a sales tax, the only way that the city can find out about your existence is if you tell them or a local store tells them. So, you can turn yourself in and buy a license whenever you feel like it. Many wholesalers may refuse to sell to you without one, but ask first. There's no sense in wasting money on a license if you can avoid it. Then again, you may be so small that the only way you will get them to sell you a license is to say that your suppliers won't sell to you without one.

OTHER PERMITS

Most suppliers are very free with information about permits and will tell you if you need one in order to handle their product. If you are in doubt, ask them. If they don't know, they probably know who to ask and will be able to find the answer for you faster and more accurately than you could do by yourself. And if officialdom gives your supplier a wrong answer for you, you will have a witness that the mistake was made at city hall and not by your conspiracy.

Having permits isn't so bad really, once the shock of being official is over. You can even enjoy flaunting your legality to get discounts on everything listed under wholesale in the yellow pages. You can pay the same prices that stores pay for the merchandise that they sell on their shelves. Always list your business as selling groceries, housewares and sundries. This will enable you to buy appliances, car parts, stationery supplies and, of course, food at wholesale prices. You might also want some fancy stationery with a letterhead, in order to seem official when dealing with bureaucrats and big businesses.

It is impossible for people to order anything without knowing what is available and what items cost. Therefore, order forms and lists are important. For a small group lists can be made by hand and the members could make their own copies. Or, the drafter of the original could make multiple copies at one time with carbon paper. Beyond five copies this technique begins to fade. You could draft two originals and thereby get 10 copies, but any more than this calls for technology.

Your local school probably has a ditto machine; a local church, club or political group may have a mimeograph machine. Find out. If such machines are available, don't make a pig of yourself. Buy your own ink, paper and stencils or ditto masters. Here is where your permits come in handy. You should get at least a 20 percent discount below retail store prices from a stationery-supply wholesaler.

For those who hate to type stencils, Gestetner has invented an electrostencil machine. If there is one of these available to you, you are in luck. (Many OEO projects have this equipment.) With this machine you can have an electric stencil made from handwritten or typed work; even pictures can be reproduced. You can simplify the job by taking an old order form and painting or cutting out the old prices and putting in the new ones. You can also cut out items you no longer want to list and write in new ones. This altered copy can be used to cut a new stencil without retyping.

You can go one step further if you have access to a key punch and a listing machine. You can punch a card for each item, run the cards through the lister and then take the printout form to the electrostencil machine. You will also have the added benefit of a self-duplicating deck of item cards. (See Grains.) You can then change an order form by adding or removing cards from the deck. You can change prices merely by changing the appropriate cards. The listing machine will do your retyping.

KEEPING RECORDS

Don't forget to include a column for price changes on your order forms. This column is a warning to members that prices do change and it is an easy place to recalculate bills if necessary.

An order list should contain all possible information which might help the member who will be filling it out. It should contain:

• The name and phone number of a member who can answer questions about ordering.

• The suppliers for the items on the list. These can be coded with a letter.

• What work will be required of those who order.

• An explanation of any oddities about ordering; for example, the fact that although members may order four-ounce units of a given spice, the conspiracy will not buy it until a pound is ordered and prepaid.

• When and where the list should be turned in.

• A statement that all orders are "cash in advance."

• Any markup which the order will need.

ACCOUNTING   When your volume gets over $20 a week, you will need a simple accounting system. Anybody can weigh out five pounds of flour, but just as there are bad drivers, there are bad bookkeepers. Not everyone is suited to keeping books and it can become boring. If you rotate the job frequently, with one member showing another how to do it, you will quickly turn up the people who do not have a knack for accounting. The person following an inept accountant will notice adding errors and be aware that his predecessor wasn't suited for the job. Those who can't do accounting (and you don't know until you've tried) should be weeded out of that rotation and given a choice of other jobs. The signature on the checking account, however, should not be rotated; changing signatures at the bank would be too much of a nuisance.

A checkbook provides the bare minimum of an accounting system. If you are getting more than one type of food, you will need to keep separate master lists for each food; i.e., one for cheese, one for produce, one for caselot, etc. These need not be a complicated six-column accounting. Two columns, "money in" and "money out," plus a column to keep track of stockpiled inventory should do the job. On each master list the following information should be recorded.

• List exact amounts paid by members and the date of payment (12/1/73 Mary $3.00 for 10 quarts milk). Have each member fill out an order form; the accountant merely adds up the total paid in on all the forms and records this total on the accounting sheet. Keep order forms in a file folder until merchandise is received.

Russell St. Food Conspiracy
Bulk Food Order Form

Name *Mary*
Address *5901 Juniper St. #4*
Phone *123-4567*

Vehicle *Panel Truck*
Food will arrive: June 19, 1972

Item	Listed Price	Amt.	Cost	Actual Price	Final Cost
oatmeal	.10/lb	2	.20	.09	.18
sh. grn. brn. rice	.29/lb				
bulgur	.18/lb	3	.54	.18	.54
cornmeal	.10/lb				
molasses,blackstrap	.75/qt	1	.75	.60	.60
barley	.10/lb				
rice bran	.09/lb				
carob powder	.50/lb	1	.50	.50	.50
soy oil	1.00/qt	1	1.00	1.00	1.00
gluten flour	.39/lb				
whole wheat flour	.15/lb	10	1.50	.16	1.60

Total $4.49
5% Markup .22

Total Amt. Paid $4.71

Total Cost $4.42
5% Markup .22

Total Amt. Due 4.64

Total Amt. Paid 4.71

Balance Due or Owed .07

- Exact amounts paid to suppliers, along with the date and a description of the purchased items (12/3/73 Max's Dairy $300.00 milk, cheese, by-products).
- Keep track of stockpiling and inventory on the master list. Cheese in a refrigerator is just as valuable as cash designated for buying cheese. If, however, you forget about three pounds of Swiss cheese and buy another five-pound block when three pounds are ordered, you will lose money through molding.

Before you deposit money into your bank account, make a list of the members' names, amounts, check numbers and ABA numbers on each check and the serial numbers on all bills. This bit of busy work will make life a lot easier for your conspiracy if the mail or the bank loses your deposit. Be sure that all deposits are recorded in your checkbook, so you will know how much money you have in total. The balance in the checkbook is also a good double-accounting measure with which to compare the total from the master lists to make sure your arithmetic is correct. If you do discover a mistake, that you have spent too much on cheese, for example, and do not have enough money for all the produce, you can tell the produce buyers to bring back less food that week. Do not however, continue subsidizing one section with money from another.

Add and subtract accurately, using an adding machine if possible and double check everything. Banks charge $3 to $5 per bounced check. Our central produce operation once ran up $100 in check charges from bouncing 33 checks in one month due to bad accounting.

If your conspiracy does have money problems, try to clear them up at each weekly meeting. If you should become deeply in debt, consider holding a potluck supper and charging 25 or 50 cents per head.

Accounting is, at best, a nuisance. You should, however, treat your conspiracy's books even more carefully than your own. If you bounce a check to a supplier, he will not only refuse to sell to you in the future, he will probably also refuse to sell to other conspiracies, too. So, in a very real sense your bookkeeping is an ambassador for conspiracies throughout your community. If you get the reputation of always picking up and paying for your food on time, you will have accomplished half the battle of keeping your conspiracy alive. The other half is getting your members to do the work and that includes accounting.

Index of Recipes

Azuki-bean meat substitute, 110
Alfalfa seed sprouting, 115
Almond dessert, Chinese, 45
Anchovy tomato marinade, 74
Antipasto, Brenda's, 18
Apples, marigolded, 124
Apple cake, Irene's, 99
Apple juice, hot spiced, 122
Apricot mincemeat, 116
Apricot nut bread, 117
Apricot, pecan, coconut drop
   cookies, 118
Arabic pocket bread, 92
Artichokes, 23

Babootie, 65
Baked beans, Louise's, 111
Banana and date chutney, 116
Banana bread, nutty, 93
Banana cake, Mrs. Curto's comes
   to Berkeley, 98
Barbecued chicken wings, 60
Basil sauce, 122
Beans
   azuki-bean meat substitute, 110
   chili, 111
   cooking most beans, 106
   dahl of yellow split peas, 109
   deep-fried peas or soybeans, 110
   do-it-yourself tortilla salad, 107
   humous, 106
   Indian dahl, 109
   Louise's baked beans, 111
   Middle Eastern lentil soup, 107
   peanut-lentil stew with
     poppy-seed sauce, 111
   red and yellow bean salad, 107
   refried beans, 109
   soy spread, 106
   spicy garbanzo balls, 110
   sprouting beans, 106
   Tunisian lentils, 110

Beef
   beef or lamb kedgeree, 66
   cabbage rolls, 70
   dried fruit, roast beef and rice, 67
   Flieg's goop à la Hollander, 70
   gereusch, (Swabian stewed lungs
     and heart), 71
   lasagne, 69
   leftovers creole, 67
   meat-stuffed pumpkin, 69
   minted meatballs, 123
   overnight roast, 66
   red cooked main course, 66
   squash stew, 67
   tamale pie, 71
   tongue in wine sauce, 71
   vitamin A stew, 67
   yummier-than-expected meat-
     loaf, 70
Beef or lamb kedgeree, 66
Beet borshch, whole, 18
Biscuits, see muffins
Bonita or salmon salad
   sandwich, 75
Borshch, whole beet, 18
Bread pudding, divine, 45
Breads
   African spice bread, 124
   apricot nut bread, 117
   Arabic pocket bread, 92
   butterhorn rolls, 94
   cornbread, 91
   Criss' crunchy carob bread, 92
   Elizabeth's whole-wheat sesame
     crackers, 117
   health bran, 93
   Ida's cranberry-nut bread, 92
   kulich (Russian Easter bread), 93
   matzos, 94
   nutty banana bread, 93
   oatmeal bread, 91
   pumpkin bread, 91
   sourdough starter, 97

Buckwheat groats, how to cook, 86
Buckwheat groats, sweet and sour, 87
Buckwheat noodles, Asian, 87
Bulgur wheat salad, 21
Butterhorn rolls, 94
Buttermilk cooler, 44
Butterscotch oatmeal cookies, 100

Cabbage rolls, 70
Cabbage soup, Greek, 21
Cakes
   date cake, 117
   ferocious cheese cake, 46
   Irene's apple cake, 99
   Jean's whole-wheat orange cake, 99
   Mother Trucker's strange cakes, 98
   Mrs. Curto's banana cake comes
     to Berkeley, 98
   sour cream cake, 46
   sourdough chocolate cake, 97
   spice cake, 124
   tomato soup cake, 99
Candy, raw, or fruit nut balls, 117
Carob bread, Criss' crunchy, 92
Carob drink, 44
Carrot paprika tzimmes, 23
Carrot raisin tzimmes, 23
Carrot ring, baked, 29
Carrot soup, 19
Cauliflower quiche, 27
Cheese dishes
   cheese and olive no-bake casserole,
     41
   cheese soup, 38
   chicken leg pie, 27
   cottage queaze, 39
   Desmid's cottage cheese flower
     salad, 38
   fondue, 43
   health-nut pizza, 40
   hellzapoppin, 40
   high-protein cheese soufflé, 43
   high-protein omelette, 53
   macaroni with cheese, 43

mamaliga (cornmeal pudding), 88
Parmesan soup, 74
pickle omelette, 53
ricotta pancakes, 43
Rink's cheese lunch, 41
rizzoto, 60
spinach pie, 28
Swiss cheese pie, 41
Cheese and olive no-bake casserole, 41
Cheese and spud soup, 38
Cheese cake, ferocious, 46
Cheese custard, 51
Cheese soufflé, high-protein, 43
Cheese soup, 38
Chicken
    baked chicken with wheat germ, 54
    barbecued chicken wings, 60
    Berkeley chicken with tarragon
        gravy, 57
    chicken Ayala, 54
    chicken breasts à la Suisse, 59
    chicken gizzard stew, 60
    chicken India, 59
    chicken soup, 50
    curry from leftover chicken, 56
    egg drop soup, 50
    fowl pineapple, 57
    gar doo gai (Chinese chicken
        salad), 59
    Hillegass spiced rice and raisins, 57
    hot (optional) chicken stew, 55
    Indian chicken with peaches, 56
    Jean Keith's dirty rice, 61
    leftovers creole, 56
    Ms. Rosemary Paprika's chicken, 54
    orange juice chicken, 56
    overnight chicken, 57
    peanut butter chicken, 55
    piroshki, 60
    red cooked main course, 66
    rizzoto, 60
    San Antonio Road chicken, 55

tamale pie, 78
Tijuana soup, 50
Tunisian chicken, 54
Walt's chicken liver soup, 50
Chicken Ayala, 54
Chicken breasts à la Suisse, 59
Chicken gizzard stew, 60
Chicken India, 59
Chicken leg pie, 27
Chicken liver soup, Walt's, 50
Chicken soup, 50
Chicken wings, barbecued, 60
Chili, 111
Chocolate cake, sourdough, 97
Chocolate mousse, 61
Chutney and mincemeat
    apricot mincemeat, 116
    banana and date chutney, 116
    dried fruit chutney, 116
    green tomato mincemeat, 29
Cinnamon tea, 125
Cookies
    apricot, pecan, coconut drop
        cookies, 118
    butterscotch oatmeal cookies, 100
    Criss' crazy macaroons, 118
    filbert cookies, 118
    forgotten torte, 61
    gingerbread cookies, 102
    ginger-vanilla curls, 110
    hamantaschen (poppy seed-filled
        cookies), 118
    honey kisses, 101
    marguerites, 61
    Mexican wedding cookies, 99
    molasses crackers, 101
    "parents," 102
    pecan cookies, 118
    persimmon cookies, 100
    snickerdoodles, 101
    sour cream joy balls, 46
    strudel, 103
    Swedish spice cookies, 102

Cornbread, 91
Cottage cheese flower salad,
    Desmid's, 38
Cottage queaze, 39
Couscous, 65
Crackers, molasses, 101
Crackers, whole-wheat sesame, 117
Cranberry bread, Ida's, 92
Cucumber soup, jelled, 19
Curried lamb chops, 64
Curry from leftover chicken, 56
Curry, lamb, 64
Custards, see puddings

Dahl, Indian lentil, 109
Dahl of yellow split peas, 109
Date cake, 117
Desserts, see also cakes, cookies,
    pies, puddings
    candied fruit peel, 118
    Chinese almond dessert, 45
    chocolate mousse, 61
    Mr. Petroff's paska, 44
    orange juice chiffon, 61
    paska, 44
    raw candy or fruit nut balls, 117
    real strawberry ice cream, 44
    Sirova paska, 44
Dressings for salads
    creamy Italian dressing, 122
    Moraga Hill Parmesan dressing, 38
    nasturtium sauce, 122
    vinaigrette, 123
    zappo for vegetables, 122
Dried fruit chutney, 116
Dried fruit, roast beef and rice, 67
Drinks
    apple juice, hot spiced, 125
    buttermilk cooler, 44
    carob drink, 44
    cinnamon tea, 125
    garden tea, 125

Index of Recipes

Egg dishes
  egg drop soup, 50
  egg foo yong, 51
  high-protein cheese soufflé, 43
  high-protein omelette, 53
  pickle omelette, 53
  quick dinner eggs, 53
  restuffed eggs, 50
  ricotta pancakes, 43
  scrambled eggs plus, 51
  Selina's high-protein pancakes, 88
  soybean egg soufflé, 53
  sweet and sour eggs, 53
Egg drop soup, 50
Egg foo yong, 51
Eggplant stuffed with lamb, 65

Felafel (spicy garbanzo balls), 110
Filbert cookies, 118
Fish
  always juicy salmon steaks, 78
  anchovy tomato marinade, 74
  fish chunks aux fines herbes, 78
  fish feast, 77
  fish kedgeree, 74
  fish with red sweet and sour
    slurpy sauce, 76
  fish with tahini sauce, 76
  halibut horn eye, 77
  Lillian's West Coast gefilte fish, 75
  Parmesan soup, 74
  polenta enough, 77
  rolled sole, 76
  salmon cake or cakes, 78
  salmon or bonita salad sandwich, 75
  tangy fish soup, 74
  tickle-tummied fish, 78
  tuna fish salad, 75
Fish chunks aux fines herbes, 78
Fish feast, 77
Fish kedgeree, 74

Fish soup, tangy, 74
Fish with red sweet and sour
  slurpy sauce, 76
Fish with tahini sauce, 76
Fondue, 43
Fruit chutney, dried, 116
Fruit nut balls, 117
Fruit peel, candied, 119
Fruit popovers, 94

Garbanzo balls, spicy, 110
Garden tea, 125
Gar doo gai (Chinese chicken salad), 59
Gefilte fish, West Coast, 75
Gereusch (Swabian stewed lungs and
  heart), 71
Gingerbread cookies, 102
Ginger-vanilla curls, 100
Goop à la Hollander, 70
Grains, how to cook, 86
Granola, 115
Green tomato mincemeat, 29
Guacamole, 18

Halibut horn eye, 77
Hamantaschen (poppy seed-filled
  cookies), 118
Hellzapoppin, 40
Herbal tea, what to do with
  leftover, 125
Honey custard, Mexican, 45
Honey kisses, 101
Hot sauce, Sharyn and Dave's, 101
Humous, 106

Ice cream, real strawberry, 44
Icing, super, 97
Italian dressing, creamy, 122

Jelly, mint, 125

Kedgeree, beef or lamb, 66
Kedgeree, fish, 74
Kim chi, Korean, 18
Kulich (Russian Easter bread), 93

Lamb
  babootie, 65
  beef or lamb kedgeree, 66
  couscous, 65
  curried lamb chops without
    a sauce, 64
  fast disappearing leg of lamb, 64
  Greek cabbage soup, 21
  lamb curry, 64
  long-cooking eggplant stuffed
    with lamb, 65
  Middle Eastern lentil soup, 107
  sweet lamb chops, 64
Lamb curry, 64
Lasagne, 69
Leek and potato soup, 19
Leftovers creole, 67
Leg of lamb, fast disappearing, 64
Lentils
  Indian dahl, 109
  Middle Eastern lentil soup, 107
  peanut-lentil stew, 111
  Tunisian lentils, 110

Macaroni with cheese, 43
Macaroons, Criss' crazy, 118
Mamaliga (cornmeal pudding), 88
Marguerites, 61
Marigolded apples, 124
Matzos, 94
Mayonnaise, 51
Meatballs, minted, 123
Meatloaf, yummier-than-
  expected, 70

Meat-stuffed pumpkin, 69
Millet, how to cook, 87
Mincemeat, see chutney and mincemeat
Mint jelly, 125
Molasses crackers, 101
Muffins, rolls and biscuits
    butterhorn rolls, 94
    cornbread, 91
    fruit popovers, 94
    pineapple muffins, 95
    RoRo's schnecken, 95
    sweet potato biscuits, 29
Mushroom salad, Erica's marinated, 22

Nasturtium sauce, 122
Noodle dishes
    buckwheat noodles, Asian, 87
    chicken leg pie, 27
    lasagne, 69
    macaroni with cheese, 43
    spaetzle, 88

Oatmeal bread, 91
Oatmeal whatevers, 89
Omelette, high-protein, 53
Omelette, pickle, 53
Onion pie, 41
Onion pie again, 89
Orange carrot ring, baked, 29
Orange juice chicken, 56
Orange juice chiffon, 61
Overnight chicken, 57
Overnight roast, 66

Pancakes, ricotta, 43
Pancakes, Selina's high-protein, 88
Parmesan salad dressing, Moraga Hill, 38
Parmesan soup, 74
Paska (Russian cheese), 44
Peanut butter chicken, 56
Peanut-lentil stew with poppy-seed sauce, 111

Peas and soybeans, deep-fried, 110
Pecan cookies, 118
Persimmon cookies, 100
Persimmon pudding, 30
Pesto (basil sauce), 122
Pickle omelette, 53
Pie crust, 89
Pies
    onion pie, 41
    onion pie again, 89
    spinach pie, 28
Pies, for dessert
    orange juice chiffon, 61
    pumpkin cheese pie, 31
    the real sour cream and raisin pie, 46
Pineapple muffins, 95
Piroshki, 60
Pita (Arabic pocket bread), 92
Pizza, health-nut, 40
Pocura, Florie's, 24
Polenta enough (fish and cornmeal casserole), 77
Popovers, fruit, 94
Potato and leek soup, 19
Produce main dishes
    California salad, 23
    cauliflower quiche, 27
    chicken leg pie, 27
    extremely edible zucchini and rice, 23
    Florie's pocura, 24
    garbanzabled zucchini, 23
    Greek cabbage soup, 21
    Greek salad, 22
    happy vegies, 28
    Hungarian salad chow mein, 26
    potato and leek soup, 19
    Sandi's vegeburgers, 28
    spinach pie, 28
    tempura, 26
    vegetable loaf, 123
    zucchini casserole, 27

Pudding from scratch, 45
Puddings and custards
    cheese custard, 51
    divine bread pudding, 45
    Grandma Morris' Thanksgiving pudding, 30
    mamaliga (cornmeal pudding), 88
    Mexican honey custard, 45
    persimmon pudding, 30
    pudding from scratch, 45
    snorfy custard, 61
Pumpkin bread, 91
Pumpkin cheese pie, 30
Pumpkin, stuffed with meat, 69

Red and yellow bean salad, 107
Red cabbage, 24
Red cooked main course, 66
Refried beans, 109
Rice, Jean Keith's dirty, 61
Rice, yellow, 86
Ricotta pancakes, 43
Rizzoto, 61
Roast beef with dried fruit and rice, 67
Rolls, see muffins

Salads
    bulgur wheat salad, 21
    Desmid's cottage cheese flower salad, 38
    Erica's marinated mushroom salad, 59
    gar doo gai (Chinese chicken salad), 59
    Greek salad, 22
    green salad, 22
    Hungarian salad chow mein, 26
    red and yellow bean salad, 107
Salad dressings, see dressings
Salmon cake or cakes, 78

Index of Recipes

Sauces
  all-of-a-sudden pesto (basil sauce), 122
  nasturtium sauce, 122
  poppy-seed sauce, 111
  Sharyn and Dave's hot sauce, 122
  tahini (sesame sauce), 115
  tempura dip, 26
Schnecken, RoRo's, 95
Sesame seeds, toasted, 115
Side dishes and snacks
  antipasto, Brenda's, 18
  apricot mincemeat, 116
  artichokes, 23
  banana and date chutney, 116
  carrot paprika tzimmes, 23
  carrot raisin tzimmes, 23
  dried fruit chutney, 116
  fried spinach, 23
  green tomato mincemeat, 29
  guacamole, 18
  humous, 106
  kim chi, Korean, 18
  marigolded apples, 124
  molasses crackers, 101
  oatmeal whatevers, 89
  orange carrot ring, baked, 29
  peas or soybeans, deep-fried, 110
  pocura, 24
  red cabbage, 24
  soy spread, 106
  soy walnuts, 115
  spaetzle, 88
  tahini, 115
  Turkish yogurt, 39
  yellow rice, 86
  yogurt (from canned milk), 39
  yogurt (from powdered milk), 39
  whole-wheat sesame crackers, 117

Sole, rolled, 76
Soups
  carrot soup, 19
  cheese and spud soup, 38
  cheese soup, 38
  chicken soup, 50
  egg drop soup, 50
  Greek cabbage soup, 21
  jelled cucumber soup, 19
  Middle Eastern lentil soup, 107
  Parmesan soup, 74
  potato and leek soup, 19
  spinach soup, 21
  tangy fish soup, 74
  Tijuana soup, 50
  Walt's chicken liver soup, 50
  whole beet borshch, 18
Sour cream and raisin pie, 46
Sour cream cake, 46
Sour cream joy balls, 46
Sourdough chocolate cake, 97
Sourdough starter, 97
Soybean egg soufflé, 53
Soybeans and peas, deep-fried, 110
Soy spread, 106
Soy walnuts, 115
Spaetzle, 88
Spice bread, African 124
Spice cake, 124
Spice cookies, Swedish, 102
Spinach, fried, 23
Spinach pie, 28
Spinach soup, 21
Split peas, dahl of, 109
Squash stew, 67
Stews
  chicken gizzard stew, 60
  chili, 111
  dahl of yellow split peas, 109
  gereusch, (Swabian stewed lungs and heart), 71
  goop à la Hollander, 70
  Greek cabbage soup, 21
  hot (optional) chicken stew, 55
  Indian dahl, 109

  lamb curry, 64
  leftovers creole, 67
  Middle Eastern lentil soup, 107
  peanut-lentil stew with poppy-seed sauce, 111
  San Antonio Road chicken, 55
  squash stew, 67
  vitamin A stew, 67
Strawberry ice cream, real, 44
Strudel, 103
Sweet and sour buckwheat groats, 87
Sweet and sour eggs, 53
Sweet potato biscuits, 29
Swiss cheese pie, 41

Tahini, 115
Tamale pie, 71
Tea, cinnamon, 125
Tea, garden, 125
Tempura, 26
Tempura dip, 26
Tomato soup cake, 99
Tongue in wine sauce, 71
Tortilla salad, do-it-yourself, 107
Tuna fish salad sandwich, 75

Vegeburgers, Sandi's, 28
Vegetable loaf, 123
Vegetable main dishes, see produce
Vegies, happy, 28
Vinaigrette, 123

Walnuts, soy, 115
Whole-wheat orange cake, Jean's, 99
Wild rice, how to cook, 86

Yogurt (from canned milk), 39
Yogurt (from powdered milk), 39
Yogurt, Turkish, 39

Zucchini and rice, extremely edible, 24
Zucchini casserole, 27
Zucchini, garbanzabled, 26

TABLE OF EQUIVALENTS FOR UNUSUAL
AND HARD TO GET OR EXPENSIVE FOODS

Brown sugar: Barbados, Grandma's or dark molasses or ribbon cane syrup.

Carob: Cocoa powder.

Chinese cabbage: Regular green cabbage.

Chives: Yellow or white onion.

Crude oil: Filtered oil generally found in grocery stores—soy, safflower, corn, etc.

Eggs: Powdered eggs can be substituted in many of the recipes.

Garbanzo beans: White beans.

Garbanzo flour: Whole-wheat flour.

Honey: Sorghum, ribbon cane syrup, molasses, etc.

Japanese eggplants: Small eggplants.

Kidney beans: Red beans.

Lentils: Split peas.

Liqueur or hard liquor: Vanilla extract.

Milk: Powdered milk plus water as directed on package.

Milk, non-instant powdered: Twice as much instant as powdered milk.

Millet meal: Cornmeal.

Mozzarella: Monterey Jack cheese.

Nutritional yeast: Whole-wheat flour or toasted soy flour.

Nuts: Any nut can substitute for others; so can sunflower seeds.

Pepper: White and black peppers are interchangeable.

Pero: Instant coffee or imitation coffee substitute.

Raisins: Currants, prunes or other dried fruit chopped to size.

Red wine vinegar: Distilled vinegar or apple cider vinegar.

Sea salt: Table salt.

Sour cream: Yogurt.

Soy powder, toasted: You can toast soy flour in a 250° oven or in a dry fry pan, or substitute wheat flour.

Spices: Use your judgment.

Suet: Any shortening, oleo or butter can be used.

Tamari soy sauce: Kikkoman soy sauce has preservatives, but it is naturally brewed like Tamari.

Tart green apples: Jonathan red apples.

Unsweetened coconut: Sweetened coconut; just remember to reduce the other sweeteners in the recipe.

Wheat germ: Bread crumbs; not of the same nutritional value, but they will make the recipe work.

Whole-wheat flour: Unbleached flour with 2 tablespoons wheat germ or soy flour included, if desired.

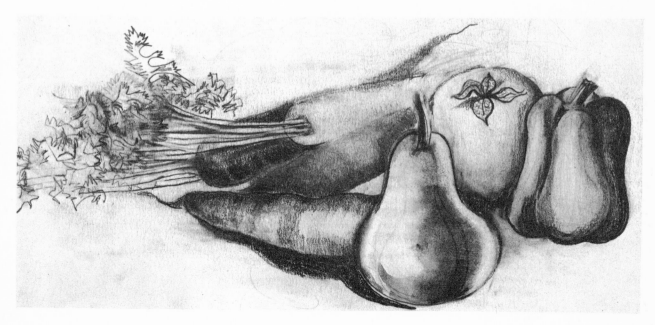

LOIS WICKSTROM

Lois Wickstrom and her husband, Eric, were among the founding members of the Berkeley Food Conspiracy, which was formed in 1969 as one of the first neighborhood buying clubs in this country. They took an active role in developing the conspiracy movement for the next three years and have continued to do so since moving to Denver with their two young children. Lois Wickstrom was born in Boston and has lived in the Midwest and in California. She attended Pasadena City Junior College and the University of California at Berkeley. Her articles have appeared in the *Christian Science Monitor* and the *Mother Earth News*. Eric Wickstrom is a biophysical chemist.

SARA RAFFETTO

Sara Raffetto studied art at the University of California at Berkeley and later in Los Angeles with Rico LeBrun. In 1961 she was awarded a Fulbright to study painting in Italy. Her work is represented in Boston's De Cordova Museum and in numerous private collections. She has illustrated two other 101 Productions' books: *Vegetarian Gourmet Cookery* and *The Wine Bibber's Bible*.